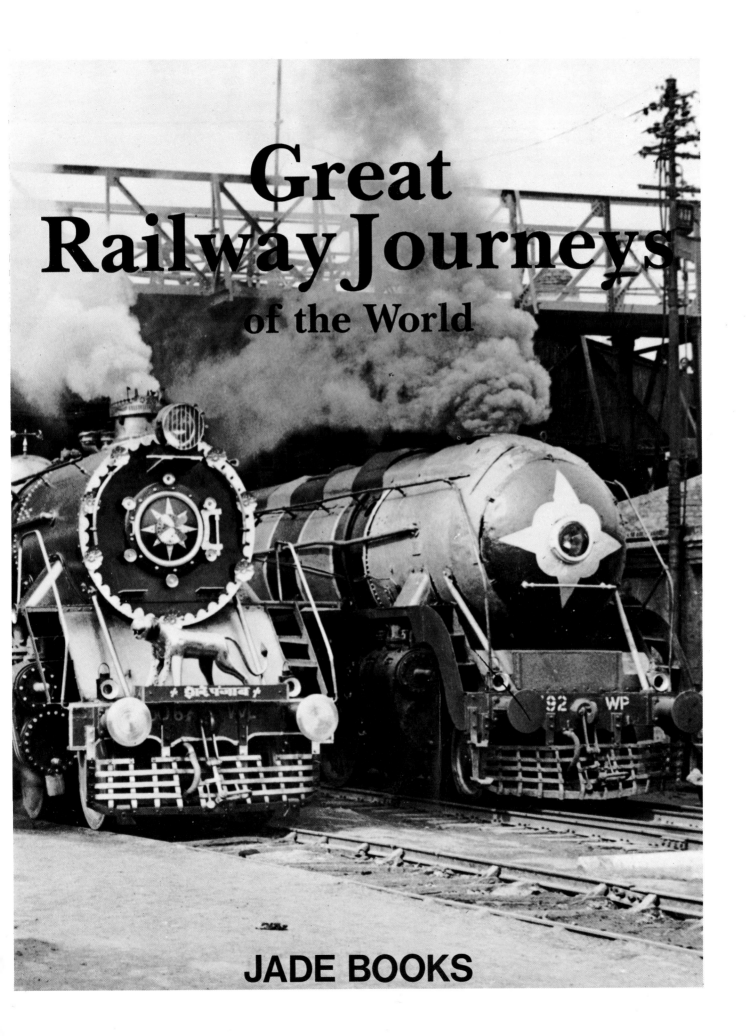

Great Railway Journeys
of the World

JADE BOOKS

Contents

Introduction *page 4*

Soviet Union *page 12*

South America *page 22*

India and Pakistan *page 42*

Southern Africa *page 64*

Australasia *page 70*

South East Asia *page 82*

Japan *page 90*

© Jade Books Limited 1983

Distributed by Omega Books Limited
1 West Street, Ware, Hertfordshire

Printed in Hong Kong

ISBN 0 907853 53 6

Why Take the Train

Collect a trunk load of travel brochures from your friendly local travel agent and you will discover that a minute fraction will include even a mention of journeys by rail. Yet rail travel compares favorably with air travel in many important ways – there are the pleasures of being able to jump on a train almost on impulse without telling anyone beforehand, of not having to be strapped in, of being able to have one's luggage with one and, finally of course, actually disembarking *at* one's destination instead of at an airfield miles outside (though it must be admitted that in the USA some of these good qualities, including the last, no longer exist).

It is also fair to say that some of the problems inherent in the world's recent social and technological 'progress' – *viz*; high-jacking, and problems brought about by unfamiliarity with sophisticated technology – affect trains less often than airliners. Trains operate more regularly in bad weather; they are also several times safer than airplanes, but this last has no real significance, for the dangers involved in either method of transport are negligible.

Nicely balanced between *pro* and *con* is the matter of eating on trains. Nothing is nicer than making one's way along the train to the diner and choosing something tasty from the menu (and remember that good food served on a train tastes superb and even moderate food tastes good). On the other hand, as the restaurant car is a separate coach, it sometimes gets detached or never put on. The airlines may offer take-it-or-leave-it re-heated food at your cramped seat, but at least the pantry is integral with the aircraft.

The main *con* in respect of travel by train is that it is rather slow. Typically, station-to-station average speeds are ten times slower than airport to airport ones. Over any distance this dwarfs the fact that railway-platform-to-city-center times are

equally typically some twenty times less than airport-runway-to-city-center ones, especially if you include time to collect baggage. The true train traveller, of course, regards the journey as an end in itself and this *con* accordingly becomes a *pro* – the longer the journey lasts, the better.

Two other things on the debit side must be mentioned. Firstly, rail travel is not normally cheap relative to air. For example, a London firm offering package ski holidays in the Alps can arrange *second-class* rail travel instead of air at around £40 ($80) *extra*. Of course, high individual journey costs can be mitigated by using the 'un-limited travel' passes issued by some countries; they are usually very reasonably priced and are valid over wide areas such as Europe, the United States, India and elsewhere.

A second drawback is that ancient reservation procedures on some railways, unchanged from 'quill pen' days, do sometimes creak a little. At A

there may be no problem in reserving a seat or berth from A to B; but try asking for a return reservation at short notice from B to A while still at A and there are – on most railways – bad problems. Accordingly sensible travel agents do little to encourage their clients to make any but the simplest journeys by rail. Fortunately not all purveyors of travel are sensible.

But all of these things pale beside the pleasure of having a behind-the-scenes look at the world through a railway carriage window. Unlike viewing the same scene through the window of a car, one does not have to drive, navigate, or superintend the driver from behind: traffic lights and jams are no longer frustrations. Without these mechanical distractions, so many interests – architecture, scenery, agriculture, natural history and so on – can be indulged in up to the hilt. It is this which makes train travel an unequalled way to travel.

Station-to-station speeds in excess of 100mph first came with these now famous Japanese National Railways' 'bullet' trains.

Pictures of the opening day of the Stockton & Darlington Railway show, behind *Locomotion*, the travellers making the best of unsprung, loose-coupled chauldron coal wagons. This would represent an extreme of discomfort, as they were unsprung both vertically (the wheels) and horizontally (the buffers). Beyond this, rancid animal fat was used for lubrication and this might spoil the enjoyment even while stationary of what was a fine day and an historic occasion.

Better things were to come – for first-class passengers anyway – when in 1830 the Liverpool and Manchester Railway commenced operations with what were effectively stage-coach 'inside' bodies in threes on four-wheeled rail chassis. This compartmented layout, ultimately with eight or more 'bodies' forming each coach, and in due time modernized with a side corridor, remained the norm in Britain and Europe until the 1960s. Early American railroads favored the open coach – which most of the world's railways have now adopted – in which the passengers sit either side of a central aisle, with entrance and exit

How Rail Comfort Developed

through doors at the ends. Rougher tracks across the Atlantic in the USA led to the mounting of carriage bodies on the now familiar four-wheel trucks or bogies as early as 1840. The present-day layout of railway carriage, therefore, evolved very early and development has taken the form of improvements rather than basic change. Stronger construction and automatic brakes have improved safety; air-conditioning (sometimes), heating and better bogies have improved comfort out of all recognition. One major improvement involved communication between adjacent vehicles. Access to and between open carriages was originally via open and drafty platforms at each end. By the early 1900s these were beginning to be made into closed vestibules and the vehicles joined to one another by flexible corridor connections. This feature is now virtually universal.

May one say as politely as possible that amongst all this, the one improvement that – from the point of view of travellers over any distance – stands out ahead of the others, is the provision of lavatories. Even before corridors came in, the best coaches had little 'utility' rooms leading out of compartments.

Not all changes were improvements; for example, during the 1850s railways in Britain stopped using coke which burns cleanly and began using coal which gives off smoke and smuts. However, anthracite coal was an improvement over the dirty-burning coal originally used. The Delaware, Lackawanna & Western Railroad once even wooed customers with such refrains as . . . .

'Phoebe says and Phoebe knows
That smoke and cinders ruin clothes,
So 'tis a pleasure and delight
To take that road of anthracite'.

(Phoebe Snow gave her name to the Lackawanna's crack express, once an excellent but by no means well-known route from Chicago to New York.) Diesel (and oil-fired steam) traction brought matters back to where they were before, but electric traction has removed even the mild residues that the burning of coke or oil produced.

In the first years of railways, passengers generally either brought their own food or snatched what they could to eat in dining rooms during stops. Similarly, they slept as best they could in carriage seats when overnight journeys were involved. In due time, dining, buffet and sleeping cars evolved to meet these needs.

The first recorded regular provision of sleeping accommodation in trains was well ahead of its general provision. There was a bed carriage on

An immigrant car on the Canadian Pacific Railway – this was the way those from the 'Old World' travelled to their new homes in North America.

the London and Birmingham Railway in 1838, while the first record of a regularly operated public dining car was on the Great Western Railway of Canada (now part of Canadian National), in 1867. Such facilities, as appropriate, are now normal on most overnight and long-distance trains the world over.

Many special types of passenger carriage have existed, such as church cars, library cars, dance cars, observation cars, gymnasium cars, bath cars, and so on, but they give pleasure to the student of quirks and curiosities rather than play a serious role in the evolution of modern passenger transport. An exception is the class of vehicles built for heads of state and other VIPs; in some countries and in the early years what was right for Kings and Queens in one decade became available for their subjects in the next.

Improvement in speed has not been an un-alloyed blessing. In some ways, a fast train gives less value (on a time basis) for money and it is certainly easier to sleep in a slow one. Further-more, by the nature of things, fast trains and spec-tacular scenery are not found in combination; this is because the only way one can build a high-speed railway through the mountains is to put it in a tunnel – and tunnels are the most boring bits of scenery one could have.

Such developments and thinking led to the Grand Hotel concept of train travel, developed in the last quarter of the 19th century by Georges Nagelmakers in Europe (and elsewhere) under the immortal title *Compagnie Internationale des Wagons-Lits et des Grands Express Européens*. In America George Pullman did the same, making his name a synonym for luxury, and giving a new word to the English language. Whether called a

Train de-luxe, an All-Pullman Limited or even a Democratic People's Express, a luxury train is required to meet the following specifications:

(a) It must be exclusive: ie, first or 'soft' class only.

(b) If night travel is involved, all passengers must be accommodated in rooms or compartments, each with one, two (or at the very most, three) beds only, made up, of course, at night.

(c) Meals must be impeccably served at tables in a dining car with *à la carte* as well as *table d'hôte* service.

(d) A buffet car and a bar car which serve light refreshments and drinks at all reasonable hours must be available.

(e) A lounge and/or observation car, may be combined with (d), for general socializing en route must be available.

The numbers of trains which met these severe standards reached peaks in 1914, 1929 and 1939, but nowadays they are rare in the extreme. It is believed that only in South Africa and Mexico can they currently be found, as regards regular overnight runs.

Nostalgia for these great trains is only partly the inspiration for this book. It is more correct to say that the theme of it is that we should admire but not weep for the past, when so many wonderful but different trains run for our enjoyment in the present.

A mixed train hauled by a Beyer-Garratt locomotive crosses the famous Victoria Falls Bridge between Zimbabwe and Zambia. Cecil Rhodes himself specified that the carriages should be washed by the spray as they crossed.

Exploring the World by Train

For those with a fair amount of time (and money) on their hands, a globe-trotting expedition by train is one sure way of finding out how the rest of the world lives. Of course, it is not possible to circumnavigate by train, and even assuming that no frontier or line is closed for political reasons, neither is it possible to make uninterrupted train journeys up and down the great land masses of America or Europe–Asia–Africa. But one can go a long way.

The longest continuous journey one could make wholly by rail is the 10,133 miles from a little-known place called Ayamonte in Spain to Ho Chi Minh City (better known as Saigon) in Vietnam.

It involves changing in Seville, Madrid, Paris, Moscow, Peking and Hanoi. Except in Vietnam, sleeping and dining cars are available on the long hauls. Bogies would be changed at the Spanish-French, Polish-USSR and Mongolian-USSR-Chinese frontiers, while passengers are still on board, to take care of differences in the railway gauge. This is fixed at 5ft 6in in Spain, 4ft 8½in in France, Germany and Poland, 5ft 0in in the USSR, 4ft 8½in again in China and 3ft 3⅜in (meter gauge) between Hanoi and Ho Chi Minh.

Ayamonte, on the southernmost point of the frontier with Portugal, is close to the south coast international resorts of the Algarve, but there is no rail connection across the river which forms the frontier. The long journey starts in the morning with a humble railcar (second class) to the famous city of Seville, with a choice of a late evening diesel express or an overnight train (first-class sleepers available) to Madrid Chambertin.

In the early evening the '*Puerta Del Sol*' ('Gateway to the Sun') express departs from the superb (but slightly inaccessible) new Madrid Chambertin Station. Paris Austerlitz is reached the next morning; transfer to Paris Nord is accomplished by the famous Metro. Again, time for a quick sightseeing trip and a meal before departure on the '*Ost-West Express*' at 1713, using the daily Russian Paris-Moscow sleeping car. There is no dining car on this train before it reaches Berlin in the morning, so the suggestion is that the voyageur obtain a hurried Parisian lunch – one that does not continue after 1630 hours – and buy ingredients for a picnic for the evening. The sleeping car attendant should have the samovar in steam for beverages. Two nights and 1½ days later one arrives in Moscow, hopefully in the early afternoon. A slightly dicey connection would (if Intourist, the Russian travel and tourist surveillance agency allow it) enable one to leave – by an un-named train – for Peking at 1725 Tuesdays only. This train runs via Mongolia. However on Fridays only there is a departure at 2040 which runs via Manchuria, a 700-mile longer journey and one that at present runs through quite steamy and humid territory at the far end. Arrival at Peking is, respectively, 1529 the following Monday or 0640 the following Friday.

The Hanoi train leaves Peking in the afternoon, Tuesdays and Saturdays. If one's visas were in order arrival would be in the late evening of the following Thursday or Monday. The real *bonne bouche* comes at the end; the remaining 880 miles to Ho Chi Minh City takes four days, including overnight stops at Hue and Da Nang. The running of this twice-weekly train, although not yet quite in the absolute top league regarding speed and comfort, is very commendable, bearing in mind the almost total destruction of the line in the recent war. The only photograph which has surfaced in the West shows steam traction, a pleasant way to end a journey of almost precisely three weeks.

There is, of course, a possible southern route, extending in principle from Europe to Singapore.

But three major gaps, not now likely to be filled and each of them hundreds of miles in length, rather spoil the tidy concept of such a train voyage. The gaps are: – Kerman in Iran to Zahedan on the border with Pakistan; Dibrugarh in Assam via the Ledo Road to Myitkyina in Burma; over the Three Pagodas Pass from Moulmein in Burma to Nam Tok in Thailand, where ran the notorious, partly graded but never completed, 'Death Railway' of World War II.

West to east on the North and South American continents is commonplace to the extent that there are at least 12 possible non-demanding transcontinental routes – not forgetting the 56 mile Panama Railroad, which once charged $25 in silver dollars for the ride.

North to south in the Americas by train is a little more ambitious, and no doubt one could hypothetically buy a ticket from Churchill, Manitoba (on Hudsons' Bay) to Merida in Mexico. If one travels on to Cuidad Hidalgo near the Mexico-Guatemala frontier, one can see that the rails continue much farther south, as far as Cutuco in the Republic of El Salvador but no train connections are given across either frontier. From Churchill to Merida, however, one could travel in great comfort the whole way, since sleepers and diners run throughout. Starting in a curiously un-named train, as far as Winnipeg, the traveller can go from Winnipeg by 'Super Continental' to Vancouver, 'Pacific International' to Seattle, 'Coast Starlight' to Los Angeles, 'Sunset Limited' to El Paso, 'El Fronterizo' to Mexico City, 'El Meridano' to Merida. Scenery with a capital 'S' graces a high proportion of the 6340-mile journey.

To go further one has to do quite a lot of republic-hopping before joining Ken Mills' excellent itinerary (Page 28), describing continuous rails from Bolivia down to the extreme south-end of the continent.

In Europe-Asia-Africa, the north to south journey came very much closer to being a reality. Starting in the north of Norway at Narvik a train ferry takes the train between Sweden and Denmark or Germany. Alas, although a train ferry does cross to Asia at Istanbul, it does not carry loaded passenger cars. Again, standard-gauge railway tracks have existed and a rail formation does exist all the way from Istanbul to Egypt, but almost all the countries concerned are at present quarrelling with their neighbors. The Suez Canal Authorities, too, whether French, British or Egyptian, have always been unwilling to allow a railway bridge across their thoroughfare except when forced to during the two World Wars.

Southwards from Cairo, the River Nile provides two undoubtedly pleasant – and certainly educational – interludes from rail travel, largely in railway-owned steamers. These sectors, totalling 1200 miles, are the physical gaps in the 6500-mile route. From Pakwach on the Nile in troubled Uganda, an all-rail route exists via Nairobi, Dar-es-Salaam, Lusaka, Bulawayo, Mafeking and Kimberley to Cape Town. Through-carriages are not, however, worked across the famous bridge at the Victoria Falls ('the carriages washed by the spray' as Cecil Rhodes intended) nor at present are there any trains between Kenya and Tanzania. Also, no train or even streetcar connects the old and new stations in Dar-es-Salaam.

Perhaps these ultimate theoretical journeys are ones which no one will ever make. However, lots of people manage the elements of which they are composed; many of these, together with others, are described in a more personal way in the body of the book. But although these words have been set down only a few days, already travel across Iran and from China to Vietnam has become problematical. One must remember that although the barriers to free travel of physical difficulty, time, and cost have been largely dismantled over the last two hundred years, plenty of manmade obstacles remain. It was only during the brief Golden Age of the 19th century that these seemed to disappear.

Right:
The Bridge over the River Kwai marks the present end of track of the Thailand railway system. The grade leading from here over the Three Pagodas Pass into Burma was the notorious 'Death Railway' of World War II, on which many thousands of Allied prisoners died.

How to Travel by Train

A must for any potential traveller is a certain book of ordinary size – the 550-page monthly *Thomas Cook International Timetable of Railway and Local Shipping Services.* To a dedicated railway enthusiast the most laconic of its entries conjures up a vivid picture of some great train rolling towards the sunset.

Three years ago the press and television covered one particular non-event, the demise of the 'Orient Express.' However, if one consults the current copy of Cook's timetable, there in table 32 is set out the schedule of the 'Orient Express,' still running between Paris (Est) and Bucharest, the same termini that it connected on its first run in 1883. The media got hold of the wrong train!

A study of back numbers of Cook's timetable indicates that rail travel in the past was not necessarily better than today's. For example, the superb trains that now run between London and South Wales or Tokyo and Osaka, compare very favorably with the very second-rate ones which operated on these routes a few years ago. At the same time, the service now offered on, say, the aforementioned 'Orient Express' or between Chicago and Los Angeles is poor compared with what was available in the day of *trains de-luxe* or the 'Super Chief' respectively.

It may be noted that rail facilities can have merit in more than one way. On the one hand, many will commend a German train, say, on the grounds of its comfort, speed and observance of the timetable. On the other, a journey in, say, Paraguay, where the train's time-keeping and even its running is so erratic that the timetable is not worth publishing, may also get the equivalent of a gold medal – a puff of steam, perhaps – because of its museum-piece carriages and steam-age relic of a locomotive. The merits of both receive attention.

It was said earlier that a drawback to rail travel is the problem of making reservations. The answer? Well, if young and carefree then a night spent standing in the corridor is no worry, should the worst come to the worst. But if one is older and values one's comfort, it is unfortunate that good judgment and encyclopedic knowledge (of everything from railway practices to Saints' days and football results) are needed before one can predict with confidence whether, on a particular train on a particular day, a chance-traveller would be jammed in the corridor or spoiled for choice between a dozen empty, clean and spacious compartments.

A solution which cuts the Gordian Knot of this problem is to sample the wares of various people who offer packaged rail travel. Many firms and societies offer such facilities; mostly, they advertise in the English periodicals *Railway Magazine* and *Railway World* or the American magazine *Trains*. Thomas Cook (who began business over 100 years ago by offering excursions by train) is still in the forefront.

Three types of rail tour can be recognized. First, one put together to special order by a travel agent who is used to coping with the vagaries of railway companies.

The second type of rail tour consists of a fixed package of railway interest for a group, led by someone with some knowledge of the area to be visited.

The third is the live-in-the-train type of tour. The range here goes from old-fashioned de-luxe on Herr Glatt's new 'Orient Express' to do-it-yourself-in-a-loincloth on an Indian Railways 'tourist coach.' It is not surprising that there is a 20 to 1 price variation per night between the two. Of course, there are others at more sensible prices in between. An all-steam tour of South Africa (qv) is such a one.

The other main drawback of rail travel – the time taken – can also be mitigated by such things as a wise choice of companion(s), books, games and refreshment; and, in respect of the passing scene, a curiosity both lively and informed. Making a traveller so informed is a main aim of this book.

The last of the world's true luxury trains – SAR's celebrated 'Blue Train' from Cape Town nears Johannesburg behind a pair of the 3340hp Class 6E 3kV DC electric locomotives maintained in blue livery to haul it.

The lounge and dining car of the 'Blue Train'. The elegant styling in semi-alcoves is enhanced by the bowl teeming with fresh fruit placed in each bay of tables.

Soviet Union

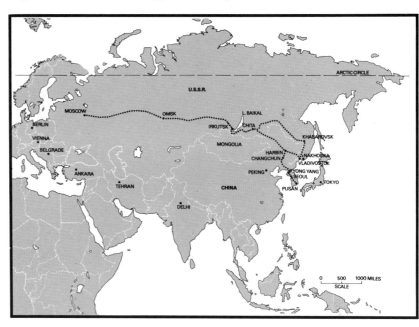

On most counts the 85,000-mile Soviet railway system is the largest in the world – unless, of course, the USA's many companies are grouped together as a single unit. In respect of freight traffic, the Soviet system does more haulage than the rest of the world put together. However, regarding the volume of passenger traffic, the system has several rivals – notably Japan and India. People in the USSR tend to be less highly regarded than freight when it comes to railroads. There certainly seems no question of enough spare capacity for people on the USSR's railways – either native or foreign – but security and custom do not allow anyone just to jump on a train. In fact, foreigners are very rarely offered any journey other than one far too famous one.

So, in following the procedure of describing a journey which illustrates the ambience of passenger travel in any country, a problem is encountered and it is this. In addition to having the largest railway system the USSR also runs a train which, by a factor of two, makes the longest journey in the world. Consequently very many travellers on what is popularly (but incorrectly) known as the 'Trans-Siberian Express,' have been unable to resist the temptation to write it into their memoirs. With this in mind, this writer feels unable to add anything to the many accounts he has read. But how to reconcile this with the fact that a piece on the Moscow-Vladivostok 'Russia Express' (that is the true name) is compulsory in any rail travel book? The solution is to set the journey not on the 'Russia' itself but through its literature.

But first a glance at the background. In the late years of the last century the rulers of Russia decided to strengthen their grip on their Siberian domains by building a railway to the Pacific Ocean. The first sod was cut at the Pacific port of Vladivostok in 1891 and through rail communication (of a sort, began in 1903. One must say 'of a sort' for three reasons. First, it was difficult enough to find the money for a railway which was longer than any which has ever been built, without adding to the burden by constructing it other than in the lightest possible way. Second, there was a gap, closed by a train ferry, across Lake Baikal and, third, the line ran direct from Harbin to Vladivostok across Chinese Manchuria.

The railway around the southern shore of Lake Baikal was completed in 1905 and the present less-direct route wholly on Soviet soil was completed in 1916. Stalin liked to claim the credit for double-tracking the trans-Siberian completely, but in fact some substantial lengths of single line remained east of Irkutsk into Khruschev's time. J P Pearson noted a lot of double-track in use and under construction in 1913. By the mid-1970s three-quarters of the railway (starting from the European end) had been electrified. A second trans-Siberian railway, further to the north and away from the Chinese border, is now under construction. From 1912 until their defeat in 1945 the Japanese operated a connecting route leading via Manchuria and what is now Korea to Pusan, a port that was specially convenient for travellers to Japan. It was all an incredible feat and, for anyone who travelled it, well worth writing about.

Below and Right:
The traditional magnificence of Moscow stations.

Both the history of and journeys on the trans-Siberian railway are well documented in Harmon Tupper's definitive account, *To The Great Ocean* (Secker & Warburg, 1965). His accounts of journeying in Siberia begin with travelling conditions in pre-railway days. The months it then took, the 'bugs,' the bad food and the unspeakable accommodation make gruesome reading. But soon after the line was opened both the Russian Government and the Wagons-Lits Company entered the fray with de-luxe trains. The Church Car that legend says was provided in fact only offered static religious sustenance for railwaymen at places along the line, while the car with baths very often did not get put on. Wagons-Lits showed some very super-special cars for this run at the Paris Exhibition of 1900, but in the end decided not to submit any but their ordinary ones to the tender mercies of Siberian conditions. Tupper includes snippets from the writings of many pre-1914 travellers. One thing has not changed – the service is highly variable from fairly good to downright awful.

A man called J P Pearson, who wrote about his worldwide travels in his monumental million-word three-volume *Railways And Scenery* (Cassell, 1932), travelled across the USSR in 1913 when things had settled down. He left Moscow at 38 seconds past 9.09 am on 30 July, calling (for example, in case you are interested) at Omsk from 3.31.12 pm to 3.49.16 pm, when 4–6–0 No 230 was replaced by No 203. Detailed stopping or passing times at most stations over most of the journey, even in the small hours, were recorded to the nearest second. His destination was Japan, so he changed at Changchun, arriving 41 minutes 2 seconds behind schedule, he reports, although very worried about his luggage at the time. He then took the Japanese controlled route through Manchuria and Korea to Pusan. Some very superior trains (of which Pearson speaks highly) ran on this line; they had been obtained regardless of cost from Pullman of the USA. They even continued running after their connections with Europe (and, hence, their entire *raison d'être*) had ceased, as Henry Carew found when he joined one almost by chance at Pyongyang.

His account (published in *The Railway Magazine* during 1952), tells of what might be called the ultimate in rail travel comfort, as the following extract indicates. . . .

I had a personal experience of the luxury service towards the end of 1916. Business took me from Japan to Korea and as far north as the town now known as Pyongyang. It was not a very pleasant place in the bitterly cold weather of a Korean November, and I was not sorry when my work came to an end. While looking up a train to take me to Pusan, on the first stage of my journey back to Tokyo, I suddenly remembered it was a Friday, the one day of the week when the special train was still running. The officials at the station pointed out that I could travel just as comfortably by the ordinary daily train at substantially less expense, and get in about five more hours in transit for my money. Moreover, my request to travel on the express meant digging out special tickets which they hardly ever used and consequently knew very little about. However, I insisted, and finally had my way.

Just before 3 pm, and sharp on time the train rolled smoothly into the platform and came to a dignified stop. It was headed by a great Pacific locomotive, cleaned and polished to exhibition standard, and followed by long, sleek carriages finished in dark green and gold. Hovering round it were a large number of young Japanese attendants in smart uniforms. As there were some minutes to spare, I walked the length of the train along the platform and it was only then I realized that I was the only passenger. The time of departure approached and the station-master stepped out of his office, came up to me and saluted, and asked if I would kindly entrain. He was followed by the Chef-de-Train, who also saluted and escorted me to the door of my sleeping car. A boy then led me down a softly-carpeted corridor and ushered me into a beautifully-furnished compartment, which he informed me was my sitting room, and indicated that the adjoining one was my bedroom; then he bowed low and left me. There was a deep and melodious note from the whistle, an orgy of saluting between the station and the train staff, and then we drew smoothly out.

Tea appeared to be indicated so I strolled along more carpeted corridors until I reached

the dining car, which I found to be a flawless symphony of ivory white ceiling, large plate-glass windows, beautiful panelling, and perfect table appointments. Here I had a choice of 24 seats, with four waiters to serve me with tea, and there was no scrimping in any way, everything was in full working order – light, heating, and flowers on all the tables. I asked the head waiter, a little facetiously I fear, if there was sufficient food to see us through to Pusan and he replied in all seriousness that there should be enough. Questioned further, he volunteered the amazing information that on every trip they stocked up with full rations for 48 passengers, and that the bulk of this was discarded at the end of the journey and replaced with fresh provisions. It was magnificent but hardly economic!

Night was closing in and the outlook became more dismal than ever. The attendant entered softly, drew down the curtains and turned on several cunningly-placed lights, examined the thermostat to see if the temperature was right, asked if there was anything which I wanted, and then withdrew. The train ran on smoothly and almost in silence, so beautifully was it sprung and insulated from all outside influence. A tap at the door and the Chef-de-Train presented himself. 'Is everything quite all right sir? Please let me know if there is anything you wish attended to. We reach Keijo (Seoul) at nine o'clock, and Pusan at seven tomorrow morning.' Then came the head waiter, complete with menu, to ask at what time I would

like my dinner. Would the *table d'hôte* be satisfactory, or would I like something cooked specially? Perhaps I would like a cocktail and *hors d'oeuvre* served in my room first? That important preliminary having been attended to by two waiters and with much ceremony, I made my way to the dining car.

The restaurant had been transformed. Blinds had all been drawn down and the place was a blaze of light with the added touch of rose-shaded lamps on each table. The dinner was perfectly cooked and served and the incongruity forced itself on me. Instead of running empty through the wilds of a desolate country like Korea the train should have been on its way, crowded with well-dressed passengers, to the Riviera, or to one of the romantic capitals of Southern Europe.

And now two of my attendants came along and proceeded to make up a most comfortable bed in the adjoining room, in which they invited me to take my rest. As this was the first, and quite probably the last, time on which I should ever enjoy the great thrill of having a special train all to myself (and what a train!), it seemed a pity to spend several hours of the time in sleep, but I had to think of the feelings of the staff, who would probably consider it incumbent on them to stay up until I had retired.

We reached the Pusan pier sharp at 7 am, after they had served me with an early breakfast in the dining car, and I was bowed off the train in great style by the entire staff.

Extreme right:
Soviet Railways' latest type of electric express train.

Below:
The Siberian scene viewed from a window of the 'Russia' express.

On the other hand, Somerset Maugham, in a short story called 'Mr Harrington's Washing,' described briefly but with shattering vividness a war-time journey (in fact based on his own experience) on the 'Trans-Siberian' proper, just as the revolution got into its stride. Mr Harrington, expostulating about lawless and uncivilized behavior, ended up (of course) just as dead as several other travellers who hadn't bothered to complain first. It is not made quite clear why Maugham was sent that way when he could perfectly well have travelled direct via Norway, Sweden and what is now Finland, as did author Arthur Ransome (famous for the 'Swallows and Amazons' children's books), who was also in Russia at that time. Ransome got away complete with spoils of war in the form of Trotsky's secretary, whom he later married – but the only trans-Siberian journey mentioned in his books is much later when the father of the 'Swallows' – Com-

mander Walker, RN – travels home from China that way and unexpectedly finds his children sailing into Flushing Harbor (*We Didn't Mean To Go To Sea*). However, it is unlikely that serving British naval officers could travel through Russia in the 1930s.

Some time had to elapse after the revolution before the line was available again to voluntary travellers although many 'political' prisoners enjoyed the line as far as Siberia in the years immediately after the revolution.

Peter Fleming, elder brother of Ian Fleming, journeyed far and wide in the USSR. Some people have all the luck, because his trans-Siberian train became seriously derailed near Chita in 1933 – the dining car and his sleeper turned over on their sides – thereby distracting the staff's attention (this was the period when station masters got shot for things like that). Fleming took the opportunity to use his camera and, hence,

those fascinating photographs published in *One's Company* (Jonathan Cape, 1934). The pictures show the pre-war Wagons-Lits cars, confiscated without compensation by the Bolsheviks in 1918.

Regarding photographs (and their confiscation), photography inside the USSR has always been a problem, and still is today. If one is caught taking photographs without permission *all* one's films are confiscated. Fleming got away with it by sitting on the films he had exposed, while allowing (under great protest) the officials to find and confiscate one containing pictures of his grandmother. It is rather grim to think that, after the book was published, these men would no doubt have been purged.

One well-known photographer, Ron Ziel, anxious in 1970 to record the superb class P-36 steam 4–8–4s, then still running east of Baikal, succeeded by using a huge press camera, built like a battleship and taking 4 × 5 inch plates. After setting this up on the platform he then accosted the most important-looking policeman and requested using his one memorized Russian phrase 'Please get the platform cleared, I wish to photograph the train.' Ziel came back with some wonderful pictures offered to us in *Twilight of World Steam* (Grosset & Dunlap, 1973). His account of taking them was published in *Trains Magazine* in July 1971. His behavior did result in his being banned from further excursions into the Soviet Union.

Christopher Portway is the only traveller of recent years who made it to Vladivostok, the Pacific terminus of the 'Russia.' Foreigners are now diverted on to the Nakhodka branch, changing at Khabarovsk, because Vladivostok is a naval base and off-limits to visitors. Portway gave his Intourist 'guide' the slip at Khabarovsk and made it to Vladivostok and back. His absence without leave from the hotel was reported, but

A Soviet Railways' class VL23 electric locomotive hauls a train into Kursk station in Moscow in 1959.

Intourist was hampered in its interrogation by having to maintain a posture of polite curiosity.

Eric Newby, who has lately written a whole book (*The Great Red Train Ride*) on the subject, also had trouble with Intourist's ambiguous role – he refers to them throughout as 'The Agency.' He did not really enjoy the journey but more because of a general sense of totalitarian oppressiveness than any real discomfort. After all, he had served his time before the mast in windjammers as well as travelling down the Ganges in a rowing boat. Even so, his account explains why some travellers enjoy themselves and others do not. He stopped off quite often and so kept changing one 'Russia' for another; one car attendant or one dining car crew would like foreigners and bother – others did not. Incidentally, around 16 'Russia' trains would be moving across the land at any one time, involving approximately 25 different crews.

Sympathizing with this attitude in his review of that book was Paul Theroux who in his best-seller *The Great Railway Bazaar*, (Penguin Books, 1974), found the 'Russia' a bit tedious to travel back on after he had travelled out east via Turkey, Iran, India and Vietnam. The catalog of writings on the 'Russia' is endless but one theme runs through them all – the pleasure of contacts with Soviet fellow-travellers, who generally feel freer to hob-nob with foreigners on trains than they do in other situations in the Soviet Union. J P Pearson was the only writer who evidently found a lot of the scenery interesting, and in his dry way recalls the excitement of seeing a virgin country being settled for the very first time. Modern writers however tend to dwell on how dreary most of the landscape is.

One traveller who enjoyed himself with huge gusto was Rogers Whitaker; he describes it very wittily in *All Aboard With E M Frimbo*, (Andre Deutsch, 1974 – written in conjunction with Anthony Hiss). His little group had a lovely Intourist lady to look after them, who brooked no nonsense with the huge useless menus (almost everything crossed off) – just insisted that they all had large helpings of caviar for breakfast. 'The caviar is fresh Caspian Sea caviar, not the salted stuff we are used to in the USA,' he says.

But of all these and many more, the writer's favorite for romance and effect is that of John Price (Editor of Cook's timetable), who describes the 'Russia' and its associated trains each month in the following style:

Soviet Railway's 4–8–4 locomotive No P36-0030 heads Train 1, the 'Russia,' about to depart from Khabarovsk, Siberia.

Table 878 MOSKVA - IRKUTSK - KHABAROVSK - NAKHODKA

TRANS-SIBERIAN RAILWAY

12 fast (N)	2 fast (B)	10 fast (D)	km	Moscow Time	1 fast (B)	9 fast (D)	11 fast (D)	Time (Z)
1st day 2035	1st day 1000	1st day 1440	0	dep. **Moskva** (Yaroslavski) arr.	1220 9th day	5 40	6 30 4th day	0
2nd day {1219	{1 16	{6 23	957	arr. **Kirov** dep.	2121	1428 4th day	1452 3rd day	1
{1234	{1 34	{6 46		dep.	2106	1413	1437	
3 17	2nd day {1549	2nd day {2028	1818	arr. **Sverdlovsk**	2106	2353 3rd day	2340	
3 32	{1604	{2045		dep.	7 08		2325	2
3rd day {1730	{6 00	{1100	2716	arr. **Omsk**	1612	9 07 7th day	9 35 2nd day	
{1748	{6 31	{1115		dep.	1557 7th day	8 50 3rd day	9 20	3
3 57	3rd day {1706	3rd day {2155	3343	arr. **Novosibirsk**	6 45	2158	2300	
4th day {4 35	{1726	{2215		dep.	6 25	2142	2245 1st day	
{1855	{7 00	{1158	4104	arr. **Krasnoyarsk**	1635	8 05	2300	
..	4th day {7 16	4th day {1213		dep.	1620 6th day	7 44 6th day	9 00	4
..	{2 46	5th day 8 20	5184	arr. **Irkutsk**	2100	1208	..	
..	2 51	..		dep.	2050	1208 1st day	..	
..	5th day {1114	..	5647	arr. **Ulan Ude**	1245	..	..	5
..	{1132	..		dep.	1228 5th day	..	..	
..	{2126	..	6204	arr. **Chita**	1 45	..	..	6
..	{2140	..		dep.	1 25	..	..	
..	6th day {2056	..	7313	arr. **Skovorodino**	1 38	..	..	
..	{2111	..		dep.	1 23 4th day	..	..	
..	8th day c 4 35	..	8531	arr. **Khabarovsk**	7 55 c erd day	..	..	
..	8th day c 4 55	..		dep.	7 30 c 3rd day	..	..	
..	8th day c 1905	..	9297	arr. **Vladivostok** dep.	1650 c 2nd day	..	..	7

Passengers travelling to Japan must change at Khabarovsk (staying overnight westbound) and continue by fast train 3/4:

	4 AG		km		FG			
..	8th day c 1825	..	8531	dep. Khabarovsk .... arr.	1110 c 2nd day	..	..	7
..	9th day c 9 40	..	9441	arr. Nakhodka .... dep.	2000 c 1st day	..	..	7

Further details are given in *The Great Siberian Route* published twice yearly by Intourist, 292 Regent Street, London W1R 7PO.

A—Runs only on day prior to sailings from Nakhodka to Japan shown in Table **1467**.
B—RUSSIA—Runs daily, Sleeping car, Soft and hard cars and Moskva–Vladivostok and v.v.
D—BAIKAL—Runs daily June to Sept., with soft and hard cars and restaurant car Moskva–Irkutsk and v.v.
F—Runs only on arrival dates of steamers from Japan (Table **1467**).
G—Sleeping car, hard cars and restaurant car Khabarovsk–Nakhodka and v.v.
N—YENISEI—Soft and hard cars and restaurant car Moskva–Krasnoyarsk and v.v.
Z—Local Time differs from Moscow Time by the number of hours shown.
c—Local Time (seven hours ahead of Moscow Time).   —The railway station at Nakhodka Port is named Tikhookeanskaya.

The Soviet Railways' class E 0–10–0 steam locomotives were once the world's most numerous type but are now reduced to a few survivors used for shunting and trip work.

South America

PANAMA CANAL

CARACAS

VENEZUELA

GUYANA

MEDELLIN
PORTO BERRIO
ARMENIA
BOGOTA
GIRARDOT
CALI
COLOMBIA

FRENCH GUIANA

SURINAM

SAN LORENZO
QUITO
DURAN
SIBAMBE
CUENCA
GUAYAQUIL

R. AMAZON

SAN LUIZ

PERU

RECIFE

CERRO DE PASCO
OROYA
LIMA
HUANCAYO
CALLAO
QUILLABAMBA
MACCHU – PICCHU
HUANCAVELICA
CUZCO

SAN SALVADOR

BRAZIL

LAKE TITICACA
LA PAZ
ORURO
COCHABAMBA
SUCRE
POTOSI
IQUIQUE
UYUNI

BRAZILIA

ANTOFAGASTA

PARAGUAY

RIO DE JANEIRO
SAO PAOLO
SERRA DE MAR INCLINES
SANTOS

ASCUNION

PACIFIC OCEAN

TUCUMAN

ENCARNACION
POSADOS

TUBARAO

CORDOBA

CONCORDIA
ALTO

VAL PARAISO
MENDOZA
SANTIAGO

PAYSANDU
PASO DE LOS TOROS
URUGUAY
MONTEVIDEO
BUENOS AIRES

ARGENTINA

CHILE

BAHIA BLANCA

SAN CARLOS
DE BRRILOCHE

0   SCALE   500 MILES

RIO TURBIO MINES   RIO GALLEGOS

Early development of railways in this vast and still partly unexplored continent was influenced chiefly by the needs of the export trades. Lines were first constructed into the interior from ports, to carry agricultural produce or minerals for shipment to Europe or North America, and in most cases it was British interests which promoted and financed them. It was not until late in the 19th century that this piecemeal pattern of individual railways began to be turned, by the construction of linking lines, into any sort of national network; and it was only in Argentina and Chile, and to a lesser extent in Brazil and Uruguay, that any kind of coherent nation- or region-wide system really evolved. In much the same way, the physical equipment of the railways, and even their gauges, were influenced at the start by local and not national considerations.

Government policies were slow to change this state of affairs. During the 19th century, governments had no choice in the matter; they had no resources to build railways themselves, and indeed were more inclined to encourage railway-building on any terms which enhanced national economic development rather than to want to do anything to influence and so retard the work of foreign capital. Quite apart from this, South American governments had the deserved reputation at this time of being unstable. But by the middle of the 20th century things had changed; nearly all the railways had, for instance, been nationalized, and foreign capital no longer had its original 'stranglehold' on the national transport arteries. Politicians were thereby much pleased; but any practical differences took longer to appear. Political instability remained endemic; the massive resources needed to carry out the modernization and redevelopment of the railways could scarcely be found. Some impressive

progress has been made here and there; but the general picture remains one of a great variety of types of equipment, of gauge, and an often inconvenient route pattern.

Nowadays South American passenger trains vary from air-conditioned luxury to spartan wood-slat seats; from thrice-daily expresses to one mixed train a week; and sweating overcrowded rush-hour suburban runs to the bitter cold of the high Andean desert. Life is supported on the way, of course; whether by the cold meat and rice emerging from the primitive kitchens of Bolivian or Paraguayan dining cars, to steak and wine in Chile and Argentina. Fares are generally very cheap, and some international rail passes are available to foreign visitors.

Northern South America offers thin fare to the railway traveller. Although Guyana once boasted the first railway on the South American mainland, no public railways now exist there or in neighboring Surinam or French Guiana. Venezuela possesses only one short standard-gauge line, first, and so far only, flower of a planned second-generation national railway system, the first having been closed down during the first flush of infatuation with the automobile. Colombia's national railway network has continued to expand, though slowly, and now comprises some 2200 miles of 3ft gauge track linking the large cities of the central provinces with a main line paralleling the great Magdalena River.

Further south, the main line of Ecuador's 3ft 6in gauge railway runs 288 miles from Duran, across the river from the main port of Guayaquil, to Quito, the cool Andean capital. Later government-built extensions added the Quito-San Lorenzo and Sibambe-Cuenca lines to complete the system. Peruvian railways consist of two distinct systems, each standard gauge with 3ft

gauge feeders, totalling only 1129 route-miles. The Central Railway links Callao port through Lima, the capital, with Cerro de Pasco, Oroya and Huancayo in the high Andes. The Southern Railway strikes inland from the twin ports of Mollendo and Matarani, via Arequipa to Puno on Lake Titicaca, and Cuzco, the ancient Inca capital. Huancayo and Cuzco are each the starting point of a 3ft gauge railway, running respectively south to Huancavelica and north to Quillabamba, the latter line busy with the tourist trade to the world-famous 'Lost City' of the Incas at Macchu-Picchu.

The Bolivian railway system totals 2240 route-miles of meter-gauge line. The western system, running on the altiplano at an average altitude of some 11,000ft, accounts for 1384 miles; the remaining 856 miles radiate from Santa Cruz, in the humid and dusty eastern lowlands. The two sections are still unconnected, except by way of a 400-mile detour through Argentina.

Chile is shaped on the map not so much like a sausage, more like a length of string. Its railway system is therefore necessarily laid out rather like a snake's skeleton, or rather the skeleton of two snakes sharing the same head. This head is at Valparaiso, the main port half-way along the length of the country. From nearby Calera the northern system, of meter gauge, runs parallel to the coast for 1160 miles to Iquique, throwing off several branches and an important secondary route from Antofagasta inland to connect with Bolivia. The passenger service on this lengthy main line consists of two trains a week, which traverse desert landscapes where no rain has fallen in living memory. In stark contrast, the broad-gauge (5ft 6in) southern system, commencing at Valparaiso and serving the capital city of Santiago, has a busy and partly electrified

main line running 782 miles southwards to Puerto Montt, again with numerous branches, all in fertile and beautiful country.

When 80 percent of Argentina's railways were operated by British companies, they formed one of the world's most efficient and comprehensive systems, and certainly far the best in South America. Since nationalization in 1949, whether or not for that reason, (though certainly Argentine politics had something to do with it), the railways became seriously neglected, maintenance deteriorated, and replacement of rolling stock fell into arrears. The fiercely competitive days of the late 19th century had left a legacy of three gauges, thousands of route-miles of now redundant tracks, and a multitude of locomotive and rolling stock designs. Partial modernization has resulted in diesel-hauled trains (some now fairly ancient) still having to struggle along on sub-standard permanent track to slow schedules.

Uruguay's compact standard-gauge railway system radiates from Montevideo, the capital and main port, along 1850 miles of line over which new Ganz railcars and older diesel-hauled trains operate rather sparse services. Speeds are slow but riding generally smooth, and the whole operation moderately well-run. A small pocket of steam locomotives lingers in the Paysandu and Salto areas.

The only public railway in Paraguay is standard-gauge and runs for 234 miles southward from the capital, Asuncion, to Encarnacion on the Parana River, connecting there with a train ferry linking with an Argentine standard-gauge railway which eventually, by means of another train ferry several hundred miles further on, gets to Buenos Aires. A thrice-weekly mixed train, operated by elderly woodburning steam locomotives, moves the traffic (though not much

A class 57 2–6–0 hauls a branch line train to Traiguen on the broad-gauge system which serves the southern part of Chile.

25

meaning can be read any longer into the words 'moves' or 'traffic') in an astonishing assortment of rolling stock. But for the hardened enthusiast, a Paraguayan train journey is one of the more highly rated railway experiences. From time to time plans are announced to electrify, and presumably to modernize in other ways, this line, but nothing has yet actually happened so far.

Brazilian railways had a similar history to Argentina's. But after a period of neglect almost as complete, reconstruction and indeed extension has been pressed forward energetically since the late 1950s. The standard Brazilian gauge is one meter, though several thousand miles of 5ft 3in line also exist, centered at Rio de Janeiro and São Paulo. Trains on both gauges are comfortable but slow, and while services between the large urban complexes are good, this is not so over the greater part of the country. But then, the greater part of Brazil consists of the largest untamed wilderness on earth.

So much for a thumbnail history of a continent's railway system. The area which they cover is so vast, the railways so disconnected, and the trains in general so slow and infrequent that it is hardly possible to conceive of any tourist ever actually making the journey we are about to describe; one would need many months to do it properly, to stop along the way and absorb something of the quite different styles of life and landscape. Serious long-distance travellers in South America fly, or if possible go by bus, over most of the itinerary. So in this chapter we must say, even more firmly than usual, that we are not seriously proposing a practical undertaking; but even so, any traveller choosing any part of the theoretically possible route will be having a rare and rewarding experience.

Left:
A class 57 2-6-0 crosses
the mile-long bridge at Bio-
Bio, Chile, with a freight
bound for Concepcion.

Below:
A Bolivian mixed train from
Rio Mulato to Potosi at
Yura is headed by 4-8-2
No 811.

It may be doubted whether anybody has ever actually travelled all the way from northern Colombia to southern Chile, down the whole length of the Andes, then swung back north to come close to encircling the whole of South America through Argentina, Uruguay, and Brazil. However, this is the journey about to be described; and maybe the description will prod somebody into doing it. About half the distance is possible by rail, and where trains exist they shall be used; alternatively, lake, river, or coastal steamers, or buses, (in that order of permissibility only). Airplanes are prohibited. Following the same absolutism, the journey shall start at Santa Marta, the northernmost point in South America served by rail, regardless of the fact that any person arriving in Columbia from abroad will almost certainly be set down first at the capital, Bogota, some 500 miles to the south.

However, the first lap, from Santa Marta to Bogota itself, is an untypically easy one, in that it can be covered in quite a comfortable, if a not very fast, daily train. The first two-thirds of the distance, along the level and near the broad Magdalena River (still plied by stern-wheelers) were actually built fairly recently, in the 1950s; trackage in the mountain districts south of Puerto Berrio is older. Bogota, on the high and cool Sabana plateau, is a well-sited city rather spoiled by some intractable social and political problems, so one is unlikely to want to linger; the way to the south lies through Cali. This could theoretically be reached by rail from Santa Marta, leaving the main line at Puerto Berrio and passing through the third city of Colombia, Medellin: however, half the Medellin to Cali line does not actually operate. So the practical route is train from

Bogota to Girardot, bus from Girardot to Armenia over the 11,000ft Quindio Pass, and then again train from Armenia to Cali. (Even more practical, and a one-day journey, but disallowed under the rules, is bus throughout.) However, the Colombian railways offer much of interest; there are still some survivors here and there of the old steam fleet, which once included some rare articulated types to cope with the very difficult curves and grades, and mountaineering curiosities like Esperanza station on the Bogota-Girardot line, which never sees a train unless the locomotive is pushing at the back, since it is situated on the center leg of a double zig-zag.

From Cali to Quito in Ecuador, some 300 miles, there is little alternative but to take the second of what will become a long series of Andean buses. A third of the distance could perhaps be covered by train, with a line running from each end towards the border, but trains on these sections are rather remote and unreliable.

South of Quito, however, on the next leg of 288 miles, the famous Guayaquil & Quito line is a very practical travel possibility indeed, and a remarkable one. The schedule offers a fast diesel railcar three days a week, doing the run in 10 hours; this may not sound fast, but with many obstacles en route it is actually a horn-blaring, dust-raising, helter-skelter rush. An alternative is to use the mixed train, trundling gently along the 11,000ft high plateau under Cotopaxi to an overnight stop at Riobamba. Next day, with 20,000ft Chimborazo the presiding mountain, one descends to the coastal plains along the famous Devil's Nose switchbacks above Sibambe, dropping 5000ft in 24 miles with a ruling gradient of 1 in 19 – and more to the point, a very good

A Baldwin 2–8–2 crosses the Magdalena River Bridge at Girardot, Colombia.

chance of seeing and being hauled by some well-maintained steam locomotives which are still at work on this very dramatic section. The final length to Duran and Guayaquil is through sugarcane fields and mango groves, across the coastal plain.

The next leg, Guayaquil to Lima in Peru, is, under the rules, a bus marathon; something over 36 hours of continuous progress, not counting an easy start in the overnight steamer to Puerto Bolivar. But recovery pauses at various towns en route, all devoid of railways (except for a few industrial short lines) are possible and permissible. Be it said at this point that roads are, in these latitudes, only marginally more common than railways. The road map of Ecuador and northern Peru is sketchy in the extreme, with basically only one north-south link; and then for the three thousand miles across Amazonia to the Atlantic coast, there is only one other north-south highway. Our snorting bus is a very rare and recent phenomenon.

The Central Railway of Peru, built between 1870 and 1893 by the American, Henry Meiggs, is certainly one of the seven wonders of the railway world. It runs from the port of Callao, through Lima, the capital city, up and over the main

Above:
Ecuador's 3ft 6in gauge Guayaquil & Quito Railway. Here a Baldwin 2–8–0 shunts at Quito.

Center left:
Ecuador's Guayaquil & Quito Railway climbs the Devil's Nose. Even though switchbacks are used, the gradient is as steep as 1 in 18.

Andes chain to Oroya and Huancayo. An important standard-gauge branch runs from Oroya to the coppermining center of Cerro de Pasco and, as mentioned, a 3ft gauge extension runs from Huancayo to Huancavelica. The main line is barely over 200 miles long but in the 99 miles from Lima to the summit in the Galera tunnel it passes through 13 reversing stations and 66 tunnels, across 59 viaducts, and runs along miles of vertiginous mountain ledges. The main passenger train now runs only three days a week, and is of course diesel-hauled but on average during the main climb taking some 4½ hours, ascends over 50 feet per minute. The train includes, of course, a dining car, and carries supplies of oxygen for passengers overcome by mountain sickness, together with an attendant to administer it. For years steam ruled unchallenged in these mountains, since no diesel could function properly over such a range of altitudes; finally General Motors developed a special turbocharger to force enough oxygen into the cylinders, and that was that. Some steam however, still survives on the 3ft gauge and perhaps also on the Cerro de Pasco line.

One must not weaken and take to the air for the next hop; it must instead be another bus epic, three days along the Andean back roads to Cuzco. But then there is another gap in the road system, one strangely enough filled by the other Peruvian narrow-gauge line from Cuzco to Quillabamba. Even apart from the considerable railway interest of making a detour along this still partly steam-worked branch, it is an essential part of any South American tour since it is the only way to get to the fabled ruins of Macchu-Picchu. One can do the journey out-and-back in a day by railcar, or by staying overnight in the hotel nearby, by steam-hauled mixed train. From the ancient city's summit, the views are unforgettable, with stone staircases, temples and terraces, clinging in breathtaking fashion to a razor-backed high ridge between two mountain peaks. White llamas graze the lawns, and tourists browse also.

The other railway at Cuzco, the Southern of Peru, is a much longer outfit than the Central, with some 500 miles of track. The main line runs from Cuzco through Juliaca to the southern capital of Arequipa and the port of Mollendo; there is a branch from Juliaca to the highest navigable waters in the world, 12,650ft high Lake Titicaca at Puno. Although it reaches heights scarcely less than the Central, and has ruling gradients that are worse (1 in 18 instead of 1 in 22, all adhesion-worked), the Southern is not so spectacular for its scenery or its engineering.

One can now leave buses behind for a while. Once a week the ancient and splendid SS *Ollanta* meets the train at Puno and sets sail for the Bolivian port (on Lake Titicaca) of Guaqui, something over 100 miles away. The rules insist on this, even though the journey is far more frequently possible by bus, but even if it is necessary to wait six days for the boat it is worth doing since (by definition) time and money are no object and the steamer is an incredible 19th-century survival of great style and comfort, even if perhaps a little motheaten nowadays. Trains

Right:
A 3ft gauge Huancayo-Huancavelica Railway railcar at Huancayo station, Peru.

The Bolivian Boat Train
leaves Guaqui on Lake
Titicaca for La Paz.

on the short railway from Guaqui to La Paz are now a bit erratic, since the railcars are rough and the mixed steam runs only occasionally. All the way from La Paz to Buenos Aires, 1500 miles of meter gauge, there is a twice-weekly passenger train. One is now really getting into civilized and populous parts. However, there is an alternative for those who have not yet seen sufficient Andean spectacle, and that is to detour from Oruro to Cochabamba by railcar, bus thence to Sucre, and back again in another railcar (or possible mixed steam) to the main line at Rio Mulato via Potosi, to see what the Bolivians can do with railway mountaineering – it does not suffer from comparison with anything seen before. Meanwhile, the main line runs across the high, arid, and rather dull altiplano plateau, actually reaching the highest points reached by rail in the world (until the Chinese get to Lhasa).

At Uyuni, still in Bolivia, one is faced with a situation unparalleled so far in this circumferroviacal tour of the South American continent; one has a choice between two all-rail routes. To reach the capital of Chile, Santiago, one can proceed either via Antofagasta and the Chilean northern longitudinal route down the western side of the Andes, or one can proceed into Argentina, via Tucuman, Cordoba and Mendoza on the original Transandine Railway. Each route is meter gauge throughout, except for the last few miles into Santiago on the Chilean main 5ft 6in gauge

system. Either way one will spend four or five days on the train, with recuperative overnight stops at Cordoba or Antofagasta; the practicalities of the choice of route are probably to be determined by the fact that there is but one train a week via Antofagasta, but at least twice as many on most of the Argentine route (Cordoba to Mendoza unfortunately runs only once a week, but Cordoba, as the pleasant city at the center of the sierras and vineyards of northern Argentina, is perhaps a better place to spend six days waiting for the next train than Antofagasta, the port serving the tin and guano industries). And scenically, a journey over the Transandine is more attractive than a trundle down the arid northern Chilean desert. Only the very rare and hardened traveller goes via Antofagasta; there are certainly bonus points of some sort to be earned that way.

South of Santiago, on the broad gauge, one is back (for a while) in the land of trains which run daily – indeed, of lines which carry more than one daily train. One should make the most of it. Southern Chile has one of the most beautiful landscapes on earth, and one of the most prosperous in South America. One leaves Santiago on electrified track; following an excellent dinner and comfortable night in a sleeping car, one wakes up beyond the end of the wires at San Rosendo to find oneself back in steam territory. Probably the passenger express will be diesel-hauled (but if the diesel breaks down, steam usually comes to the rescue), but certainly freights and branch-line trains will still be steam-worked, and by reasonably well-kept locomotives too, some of them modern. Branch lines diverge frequently towards the coast or up beautiful valleys leading towards lakes and volcanoes.

The end of the line is at Puerto Montt, some 700 miles south of Santiago; but much less than a day and a night is needed to cover this distance here, in contrast with the rate of progress till now. By this latitude the Andes, though still an impressive mountain range, have declined greatly and no longer present the same formidable obstacles that they once did. Consequently, the traveller has another choice for the next leg of his other journey, since he or she can travel either in one day from Puerto Montt to San Carlos de Bariloche in Argentina by bus or in two days by boat and bus using the chain of lakes which covers much of the distance. San Carlos de Bariloche is a winter sports and summer holiday center and is said to be Argentina's cleanest town, a distinction which means more in Argentina or Chile than it would have in some of the other countries already passed through. From here, another 5ft 6in gauge railway runs 1075 miles north and east to the capital, Buenos Aires, with a train which runs daily in summer and twice a week in winter.

As far as Bahia Blanca the going can be a bit rough and dusty; thereafter the fertility of the

country improves. One interesting detour on this section, south of Bahia Blanca, is a trip over the 2ft 6in gauge branch from Ingeniero Jacobacci to Esquel – 250 miles of very remote and rural, steam-worked and beautiful, if hardly economic, track. In Esquel and further south in Patagonia, it is still possible to hear Welsh spoken, though perhaps not quite the same Welsh that would pass in Wales today. Given time and cash one could penetrate much further south, in fact to another 2ft 6in gauge line and the southernmost railway in the world, the recently built and entirely steam-worked section from Rio Gallegos, 155 miles to the collieries at Rio Turbio, opened in 1951. Curiously enough, this outfit has never had anything to do with the Argentine Ministry of Railways since it was built and is operated by the Ministry responsible for collieries, and is chiefly notable for having the largest and most powerful, and very much the most advanced, steam locomotives ever to have run on any narrow-gauge railway anywhere (or for that matter on many standard or broad-gauge lines). Scenically, culturally and climatically, southern Patagonia can only be rated somewhere solidly below zero in any guidebook, but its steam power is one definite plus!

South America is a land of contrasts, and one of the most decided contrasts of all is the arrival in Buenos Aires along the four-track main line into the 15-platform Plaza Constitucion terminus

The weekly mixed train from Sucre to Potosi in Bolivia takes water at an isolated Andean watering point headed by Hitachi 2–8–2 No 671.

(one of many modern stations in the city). It is good to be reminded of the fact that the commuterland grind of Clapham Junction or Jamaica, Long Island, has its Latin American counterpart. Having rested among the comforts and delights of Buenos Aires, one can skip across the water (overnight steamer or hydrofoil both permissible) to Montevideo and relax again in the Uruguayan capital.

Uruguayan railways, like Argentine ones, are now recovering somewhat from a period of politically induced decrepitude, though neither have recovered sufficiently as yet to have banished all their remaining steam locomotives to the scrapyard. On the way north and east from Montevideo to Paysandu via the redolently-named focal point junction of Paso de los Toros, one is likely to see some of the survivors, though probably doing little more than shunting. More characteristic of this part of the world is the continuing sight of black-hatted and baggy-trousered gauchos rounding up their cattle. A short railcar journey on to Salto, and one crosses the wide Uruguay River to Concordia, back in Argentina (though in the standard-gauge province of it). The next train is (assuming one has calculated the day right) the twice-weekly one which carries through sleeping cars from Buenos Aires to Asuncion; the journey to the capital of Paraguay occupies two nights, beginning early on the first morning and arriving mid-afternoon on the third day.

Train ferries in northern Argentina are quite interesting ones. The ferry between Posadas and Encarnacion (Paraguay) is a particularly choice specimen, with a steam-powered haulage engine winding the coaches one by one off the boat and up the ramp, whence they are led up a switchback and along the streets of Encarnacion by a woodburning tank engine. The 231-mile main line of the President Carlos Antonio Lopez Rail-

Rolling stock of the privately owned Antofagasta and Bolivia Railway Company forms a train on the Northern Transandine Railway, Chile.

Left:
An Argentinian 3ft gauge double-headed train, northbound from Esquel to Ingeniero Jacobacci at El Maiten.

Below:
The Southern of Peru main line runs from Cuzco through Juliaca to the southern capital of Arequipa

Above:
Argentina: the British
origins of Argentinian
railways are clearly
indicated by this view of a
Vulcan Foundry 4–8–0 on a
local train at Tandil. Note
the semaphore signals.

Right:
A transandine train on the
northern route, hauled by
Henschel 2–10–2 No 1335.
This photograph was taken
from the bed of a Pullman
sleeper.

way from Encarnacion to Asuncion takes our
train 18 hours (with a little bit of luck), behind a
fine old British-built woodburning 2–6–0 of 1910;
eating in the lurching restaurant car is a little
difficult because of the tendency of the crockery to
fall out of the open window, and the tendency of
passing wildlife (mainly insect) to come in by the
same route. However, one eventually arrives at
the immaculate marble platform of Asuncion's
multi-columned station, to the sound of streetcars rattling past.

Actually, the trip to Paraguay is a detour; one
could in fact have taken the other line from Paso
de los Toros and crossed into Brazil, and then by
meter gauge and various stages to São Paulo and
Rio de Janeiro. In any case, although there is by
no means any very cohesive long-distance system
of passenger trains in southern Brazil, the route
is possible about thrice-weekly, given a little
dedication; and a very worthwhile detour in the
area is, in any case, essential, to see the quite
isolated but very fine Santa Catarina railway
based at Tubarao. This is a coal-hauling line,
the last important wholly-steam-worked line in
Brazil, and impressive in the extreme with fine
modern 2–10–4s hauling 1600-ton trains down to
the sea at Imbituba. To reach it means a side-
trip by bus, either from the Uruguay border to
the São Paulo line, or equally possible all the way
from Asuncion, in Paraguay, whence a road leads
due eastwards to Brazil. There are several other
railways in Paraguay, by the way, all running
from ports and landing stages on the Paraguay
River north and upstream from Asuncion; maps
and directories show them, but no traveller known
to the author has yet returned with any description of them and they must be regarded as subjects
for the more advanced researcher.

São Paulo is Brazil's largest city, and a modern
metropolis second to none. São Paulo also lies
near one of the world's greatest railway oddities,
the Serra Nova inclines, which carry the broad-
gauge Santos-Jundiai Railway up the 3000ft
escarpment of the Serra de Mar. Starting at
Paranapiacaba, an hour by electric train from

Above:
No 3023 4–6–2 at Santa Fe,
Argentina.

Right:
A steam-worked
locomotive as used on the
famous rope-worked Serra
de Mar inclines of the
former Santos-Jundiai
Railway in Brazil.

the Luz station in São Paulo, the main part of the heavy freight and passenger traffic on this route is still taken up the steam-worked, rope-worked, 1 in 12 inclines, seven miles long, which date back to the opening of the railway at the turn of the century. Oil-fired steam 'streetcar-type' locomotives carry grips which fasten onto steel ropes, powered by immaculate steam stationary engines, and the combination of types of power passes traffic up five consecutive inclines, on each of which ascending and descending trains have to be balanced. The complexity of the operation is considerable, but it remains in full use alongside a newly-built electrified rack railway which simply takes part of the business. Both lines are cut into a steep mountainside, with a succession of tunnels and viaducts over deep ravines.

São Paulo to Rio de Janeiro, something over 300 miles, is perhaps the most important main line in Brazil; it is broad gauge and electrified. Unfortunately the passenger service on it is not very remarkable either for speed or frequency, though the equipment is good. Perhaps this is the moment to say that Brazilian railways have a policy of doing as little as possible to encourage passenger traffic – in fact they act positively to divert as much long-distance passenger business to road as possible. However, Rio is a beautiful and interesting enough city to attract attention, with much railway interest of its own. The yellow Carioca streetcars still teeter over their impressive double-arched viaduct (originally an aqueduct), high above the rooftops, on their way into the suburban hills of Santa Teresa, and the electrified rack Corcovado Railway still takes the passenger up to the amazing mountaintop statue of Christ. And for a final steam 'fix,' one can spend a couple of days on a slow excursion to the all-steam 2ft 6in gauge line from Antonia Carlos to São João del Rei, a couple of hundred miles northwest of the city. The daily passenger train to São João, an old colonial city with two beautiful 18th-century churches, is formed of a rake of

Woodburning North British Locomotive Company 2–6–0 No 58 heads a through Asuncion-Buenos Aires train.

brown wooden coaches hauled by a diminutive but spotless 1889-built American 2–8–0, antique perhaps but still able to run fast. The narrow gauge actually continues for a total of about 70 miles, and it is possible to return to Rio by another equally interesting route.

Rio de Janeiro would be a sensible place to end our South American tour, a high spot, and one of the most beautiful cities in the world. Any dedicated traveller who has come this far deserves to pass with honor into the small, select band of super-achievers in this very special field. The sad fact remains, however, that one has so far travelled around barely two-thirds of the continent. Thus, after a brief sojourn in Rio to recuperate, one must again take to the rails.

Meter gauge rails lead north again from Rio, either to Brasilia, the Monday to Friday ferro-concrete capital plonked down by politicians in the middle of the Amazonian jungle, or further along the coast and inland alternately and indirectly to Salvador, Recife, and ultimately São Luiz, round the corner and undeniably back on the north coast of the continent. But the next two thousand miles are disastrous; practically no road for half the distance, and practically no railway either. Guyana, which once had the oldest railway in South America, now has nothing except an upstream, jungle-land, diesel-ized ore-hauler. Surinam may still have a steam train once a week, but no map of the area is of a large enough scale to show the two ends of its line as two separate points. Venezuela once had a marvellous narrow-gauge mountain line from La Guiara to Caracas, but blasted it to bits for a superhighway; they have large plans to build a new railway network somewhere else, and actually opened the first section of it, achieving within a matter of months a spectacular head-on collision. Thus, from the middle of Brazil back to our starting point, Santa Marta in Colombia, no rails exist now nor have ever existed, except locally in the Maracaibo oilfields. And so it's malarial jungles or back to Rio.

Needless to say, most visitors to South America will be forced to include airline tickets in their travel documents but any and all attempts at rail travel in this continent are rewards in themselves. No country is best seen from airports and this is particularly true of South America.

The meter-gauge Dona Teresa Christina Railway of Brazil. Here a Baldwin 2–10–2 with coal train nears Tubarao.

India and Pakistan

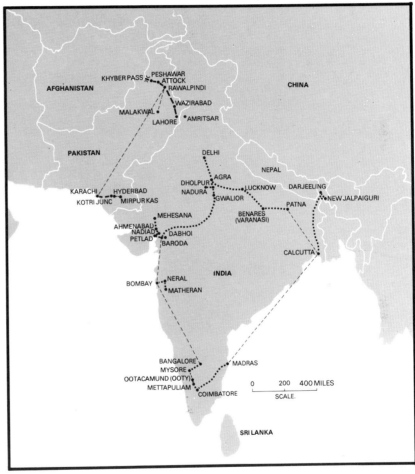

The 36,000-mile Indian rail system is by far the largest in the world to be generally open to any traveller who just simply buys a ticket. It is roughly 50 percent larger in route-mileage than the United States passenger network; in fact, the only system in the world larger than the Indian one is that of the USSR and a mere ticket does not constitute open access to the Soviet Railways. Furthermore India has by far the largest steam locomotive fleet in the world; it operates on both the narrowest of narrow and the broadest of broad gauges; and English is Indian Railways' mother tongue.

One must also consider before rushing off to enjoy India's railways that ten million passengers are carried by Indian Railways each day! Sometimes, waiting on an Indian station in company with a too large proportion of that ten million, one occasionally wishes that a passion for rail travel was a rarer thing in that country. It is significant that, for some routes and certain types of accommodation, one needs to book ahead six months and more. Similar remarks apply to Pakistan.

The writer, whose first visit to India was on his own, strongly suggests that others should not follow his example but, instead, do what he did on his second and third trips and go with a group.

An account follows, in the form of a cocktail mixture, telling of both the group tours. It contains, written between the lines, many 'dos and don'ts' in respect of Indian rail travel. The tours were arranged, respectively, by Bill Alborough, who runs tours under the name 'To Europe for Steam,' in 1975 and by Festiniog Travel in 1978. In both cases local arrangements in India were made by the Travel Corporation of India.

Nuts-and-bolts information on steam locomotives is not generally appropriate to this book, but an exception is made in the case of India, the 'steamiest' country in the world. Indian steam locomotive history can be divided into four overlapping periods. Primeval or non-standard (1852–1914), BESA (1903–1950), IRS (1926–1939) and post-war steam (1947–1972). During the Primeval period, 2–4–0s and 0–4–2s were the norm, although some lines had 4–6–0s long before such monsters were used in their home country. Broad-gauge non-standard steam locomotives have virtually disappeared, and they are very rare on the meter-gauge lines. The narrow gauge,

Bottom:
A gilded Jaguar and polished cup-type wind gauge are among the embellishments of this class WL 4–6–2 at Delhi Junction shed.

Below:
On Indian Railways' extensive 5ft 6in gauge network, two well-turned-out and rare class HSM 2–8–0s set off with a Khurda Junction to Puri train.

however, has many quaint survivors still doing excellent work.

The British Engineering Standards Association (BESA) designs were introduced in 1903, covering 4–6–0, 4–4–2 and 4–4–0 passenger designs and 2–8–0, 0–6–0 freight. The 4–6–0s were still being built as late as 1951. Corresponding 4–6–0s and other types were constructed for the meter gauge. Many BESA locomotives are still to be found working in 1978, a tribute to their sound design.

Alas, the same comment cannot be applied to the IRS designs, mainly consisting of 4–6–2s of three different sizes (XA, XB, XC), and two 2–8–2s (XD, XE). The Pacifics had a reputation of being poor steamers, sluggish runners and the XBs particularly, were bad riders to a point not of discomfort but of danger. In the end, at Bihta, in 1937, one derailed with the loss of 117 lives. An enquiry led to some modification, but the IRS broad-gauge designs never met the promises of their design committee, although some are still to be found in use. On the other hand the meter-gauge IRS YB 4–6–2s and YD 2–8–2s are satisfactory machines, while on the narrow gauge generally, the ZB 2–6–2s and ZE 2–8–2s remain the last word in steam power even today.

During World War II, Lend-Lease brought quantities of North American broad- and meter-gauge 2–8–2s to India. Their rugged characteristics showed up well in conditions there and led to an order being placed with Baldwins of the USA for the first batch of a new standard range of locomotives. So, in 1946, there arrived in India the first WP 4–6–2s. Further batches built in many countries brought the total to 755, later to be eclipsed by the WG 2–8–2s which reached 2450. There were also small WL 4–6–2s as well as three corresponding designs for the meter gauge, YP 4–6–2s, YG 2–8–2s and YL 2–6–2s. A handful of ZP narrow gauge 4–6–2s were also acquired, but insufficient for them to be regarded as a standard design. Some 40 percent of Indian steam is made up of these excellent post-war locomotives. Many were built in India, in particular at the Chittaranjan Locomotive Works, set up in 1950 with British aid in order to give India self-sufficiency in locomotive construction. Locomotive building was no new thing for India; contrary to popular belief, even in the days of the Raj several of the old companies built their own locomotives and coaches.

The once-weekly Pakistan Railways train on the Nushki Extension Railway threads uninhabited country en route for Persia. Only 150 miles separates the terminus of this line at Zahedan from rails which connect with those of Europe.

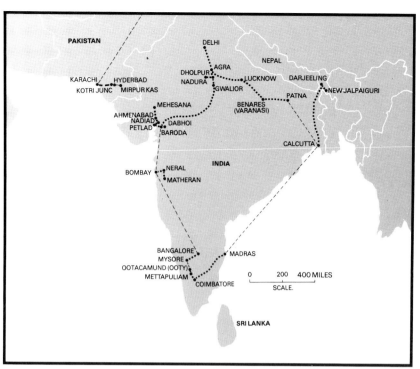

those live coelacanths of the locomotive world on the 2ft gauge at Neral, 0–6–0Ts with Sir Percival Heywood's design of flexible wheelbase system (side play on the center axle and *radial* movement on the outers). Sir Percival's creation did us proud on 45ft radius curves, which would normally be considered severe for $7\frac{1}{4}$in gauge and prohibitive on $10\frac{1}{4}$in. The first one had a big sign 'OOPS, WHAT A CURVE!' and our locomotive's way with a combination of this and a 1 in 20 grade would have done the old man's heart good. It must be noted that after *two* hours climbing Neral was still in sight far below.

Monkeys abounded in the woods round the little hill station of Matheran, where the group relaxed before departing on the booked diesel train back down the hill, steam having been specially arranged for our ascent. However, 'you

Most of us still do not really believe what we saw in this incredible land, possessor of a fleet of steam locomotives which is the world's largest by a factor of at least two. Was it only in a dream that we witnessed a decorated 2ft 6in gauge 2–6–2 being named *Mohindra* to honor a visiting Chief Mechanical Engineer with a charming ceremony that included flower-garlanding the leader and ladies of our party?

After an uneventful flight, the party's first sight of India was magnificently squalid urban Bombay, whose enterprising operators relieved members during the first few hours of both a wallet and a camera. Worse was to come, for awaiting the party leader was a letter announcing that photography of locomotive sheds would *not* be permitted. A certain blight was therefore cast over the first formal visit to Lower Parel Shed, where we saw two out of the three principal generations of 5ft 6in gauge Indian express power (post-war WP 4–6–2 and BESA 4–6–0) specially cleaned and paraded for our benefit in perfect conditions, while cameras languished under guard in the locomotive foreman's bungalow. The day was not completely lost, however, for our Travel Corporation of India coach went on to give us some excellent lineside steam picture opportunities on the Western Railway main line. TCI made all the arrangements in India, the main burden falling on their couriers who accompanied the party throughout.

The tour started with 'Matheran Monday', an outing on the Central Railway, beginning at Bombay Victoria Terminus. Indian Railways' origins are absolutely clear when one finds that the Western Railway terminus is called Central! What a pleasure to see early-electric English 'crocodile' locomotives in action on the CR main line to Poona, but it is nothing to that of finding want steam, I put steam on' was the station-master's reply to someone's diffident enquiry and so it was. Good news awaited our return, in that having carried the matter as far as Delhi, it had been established that the ban on photography would not apply to steam locomotives but only to their installations.

Tuesday morning was devoted to a rarely granted privilege, a visit to the Bombay Port Trust's elegant steam power (Vulcan/Nasmith-Wilson 2–6–0Ts in use plus stored 2–10–2Ts), followed by a rather more productive visit to Lower Parel Shed, a rapid but excellent lunch at Hotel Transit near the airport and lastly an Indian Airlines flight north to Ahmenabad, the capital of Gujerat State.

'I wonder what they feed it on' said someone as we contemplated the disreputable local bus

laid on to take the party to the pleasantly oriental Cama Hotel for the usual brief night before 'Meter Gauge' Wednesday. However, the orientality of the hotel did not prevent it from serving porridge with its pre-dawn breakfast and, after a few mouthfuls, instantly it became broad daylight. Sabermarti Junction Shed was the first call and, for most, it was also the first sight of the huge meter-gauge network, 16,000 miles in extent – on its own 50 percent larger than British Rail – which rivals the broad gauge in size but which is really very little known. We met the very fine scaled-down versions of Indian standard broad gauge locomotives (YP 4–6–2, YG 2–8–2, YL 2–6–2) plus a good collection of interesting older types, including some 4–6–0s, 4–6–4Ts, and, my wife was delighted to note, some YB 4–6–2s, products of her home town of Darlington.

An Indian 2ft gauge 0–6–0T locomotive hauls a train from Neral. These locomotives can negotiate 45ft radius curves.

The gateway to Indian
Railways – Victoria
Terminus, Bombay.

The next event was a 60-mile meter-gauge ride
north to Mehesana behind a YP 4–6–2 in two
special first-class reserved bogies marshalled at the
front. Double track stretched across the plains of
India, the wide spacing proportionate to the
gauge reminding one of the Romney, Hythe &
Dymchurch Railway in Kent, England, just as
the YP did in following Henry Greenly's narrow-
gauge proportions. It was wonderful to look out
and see traditional British-style lower-quadrant
semaphores – distant, home, starter pulled off at a
nice angle for us at each station – and occasionally pass other steam coming the other way.
Mehesana and another big locomotive shed, into
which we were taken complete with our bogies,
came all too soon. Finally, after superb locomotive viewing and train watching there, we
were *attached* to an immense 20-coach diesel-
hauled '1 Down' 'Delhi Mail' to return to
Ahmenabad, perhaps just a trifle jaded after a
very long and rather hot day. No bus appeared to
take us back to the hotel, but instead, a fleet of
two-seat motorized three-wheel rickshaws; spirits
rose as we raced through the packed city streets to
dinner and the odd hour or so in bed.

More pre-dawn porridge and we were off by
electric train to Nadiad where the shed had all

the charm of narrow-gauge independence, for these 2ft 6in gauge railways were, until a few years ago, the personal property of a very great rail fan, HRH the Gaekwar of Baroda. A Yugoslavian-built standard ZB 2–6–2 and an old Bagnall 0–6–4T were swung on the table in the sunshine for us, while we in our turn provided entertainment for the local population, as well as their animals. At all the sheds we went to, the viewing of locomotives was followed by kind hospitality in the form of welcome cups of tea, together with particularly interesting conversations on the best of all subjects. Nadiad was specially nice as we sat in the shade of a creeper-covered loggia watching Indian squirrels frisking around in the foliage.

Soon it was train time and the Bagnall was nosing across a lozenge (rather than a diamond) crossing over the broad gauge with a big packed train and we became part of the countryside in the way road transport never does. One rubbed one's eyes to see wild peacocks wandering in the fields and then, wonder of wonders, a run-past . . . and on a service train, too. The only problem was that lots of the other passengers descended and ran past with the train too. After a meet with a ZB (nice Old English semaphores again), Petlad came all too soon. A WL light standard 4–6–2 took us on the broad gauge to Anand for a shed visit and lunch in the first-class ladies and gents waiting rooms, made co-ed for this occasion. Incidentally, a sidelight on Indian social conditions is that first-class fares are approximately six times the second class, the latter being modestly set at around $2 (£1) for 200 miles.

We travelled electric to Baroda, with a stop short of the station for the party to descend,

cross running lines and a hump yard with humping in progress, to visit the shed. Nicely polished standard types, plus a superb and quintessentially British BESA 4–6–0, gleamed in the now ideally angled sunshine; then we transferred, once again by rickshaw at a high speed, to our Hotel Utsara to get, for once, a nice early night in preparation for one of the red-letter days of the tour, 'Dabhoi' Day. The Chief Mechanical Engineer of the Western Railway, Mr Mohindra Singh, honored us by deciding to take the opportunity of making a visit to Dabhoi on the day we were due there. Dabhoi is a meeting point of five 2ft 6in gauge branches, all once part of the princely Baroda system and has forests of traditional lower quadrant semaphores and British-type fully gated level crossings. These really came into their own as a hurly-burly of ox and camel carts, livestock and people, whose appearance could hardly have changed since Biblical times, poured across. It also has a shed with an allocation of over 30 ZBs, plus 4–6–0s and 2–8–4Ts.

However, when the great man arrived, everything went well and after a dignified forehead daubing and garlanding ceremony, a curtain was pulled back to reveal a ZB whose dazzling décor made the eyes blink. Fretted brass plates shone in the sunshine and such touches as a duck or dove silhouetted on the chimney and a revolving wind-gauge on the dome told of a dedication to and a love of steam which made us take Dabhoi Shed and its staff to our hearts: and they named the engine *Mohindra* to honor their chief.

One might think anything else would be an anti-climax, but not so, for miniature fans anyway, because in the afternoon we came upon a real lost treasure, the ex-Surrey Border and

India's meter-gauge system: standard class YP 4–6–2s 2448 and 2499 cross at Kaparpura.

49

Camberley Railway miniature 10¼in gauge LNER Pacific built by tragic Charles Bullock in 1938 for that ambitious but only briefly existing line. She was hard at work in the municipal park (previously the Palace grounds), having been lost without trace for some 35 years. Footplate riding (yes, literally) was also indulged in nearby on some elephantine 0–1–1–1–1–0s with an extremely heavy axle-load rating.

On the following day, a few members and ex-members of British Rail staff with the group (including the writer) were treated to a tour of the Indian Railway Staff College, previously the Royal Heir's Palace. 'We have re-organized today's program so you can give us a talk,' said the Principal over coffee amidst the painted animals on the walls of what had once been the Royal Nursery. However, all must be forgiven, for we were then shown what must be one of the most wonderful model railways in existence. There were 23 working signal boxes, fully interlocked with proper block or tablet instruments, set out in a great hall with track (about 2in gauge) and complete signalling, representing all the kinds of railway working to be found on Indian Railways. A trick was missed, I think, for those of the party to indulge in the no doubt humbling experience – for self-styled railway experts – of working the layout.

The party then regrouped to travel overnight to Delhi. Long distance travel by rail in India is what might be called an acquired taste and few had a comfortable night. In mitigation, although the train was diesel hauled, steam was visible in the moonlight almost whenever one looked out. But, on arrival at Delhi, real beds in the Hotel Akbar never seemed more inviting. Duty, however, drove us out sightseeing; most memorable of the sights were the Lutyens' Government Buildings in New Delhi. The next day, also in New Delhi, there was an opportunity to see the superb railway museum, created by another Englishman, Michael Satow, who is currently engaged in organizing the Inter-City 150 jamboree in Britain. The 2–2–2 *Fairy Queen* of 1870 to the Bengal-Nagpur 4–8–0 + 0–8–4 Garratt of 1935 delineates the range of a collection which magnificently represents Indian railway development, apart, that is, from some notable absentees which will be available when they finally go out of use in a few years.

At Delhi shed, the staff had vied with Dabhoi in decorating an old inside cylinder BESA 0–6–0 and a modern WL light 4–6–2. The latter included

India's narrow-gauge system: a standard class ZB 2ft 6in gauge 2–6–2 at Nadiad.

in its décor a golden Jaguar in front of the smokebox.

The next morning at 0645 hours and in spite of being under the bows of the flagship, the driver of the 43 down 'Taj Express' saw no reason why members of the party should not ride with him on his 4–6–2 and in this way Agra was reached by mid-morning. May one say that the beauty of the Taj Mahal is such that it took away any thoughts of steam and all voted to return that evening to see it again in the moonlight. Add the fact that Clark's Shiraz Hotel had a resident elephant available for rides and one can imagine that railways for one short half-day at least took a back seat.

The next day was 'Dholpur' day. If Dabhoi in far off Baroda represents large scale narrow gauge, Dholpur, south of Agra, is the headquarters of a pocket-size 2ft 6in system. It has a wonderful Boston Lodge style works (Boston Lodge is the repair shop of that grand-daddy of all narrow gauge, the Festiniog Railway) in which ageing 2–8–4Ts from Hunslet of England and 4–8–0s from Hanomag of Germany are put into order, while rolling stock is built from scratch. The group's accommodation on the 10.45 train included the old Maharajah's saloon and the group's depleted numbers, after allowing for those AWOL on their way to the delights of

the 2ft gauge in Gwalior, 40 miles to the south, could just be accommodated. The bus which had brought us to Dholpur met the train at Napura station down the line.

The special first-class bogie attached that evening for us to the 'Avadh Express' for Lucknow (steam, electric and diesel traction in succession) had had less than a first-class cleaning; although, to compensate, the rolls of bedding (complete with towel and inflatable pillow) in their canvas covers were brand-new. Lucknow had temples, broad and meter-gauge sheds (including BESA 4–6–0s and a rare IRS WM 2–6–4T) and, of course, a Residency, still lovingly cared for under Indian Independence more than 120 years after the famous siege was lifted.

Lucknow to Varanasi was a daytime ride; marshalled next to the group's special bogie was an Indian Railways second-class Tourist Car, in which a party (organized by Butterfield's Tours of Leeds, England) was living while rolling by rail round India. Accommodation was primitive with wooden do-it-yourself bunks and a cast-iron coalburning range, on which a cauldron of homemade marmalade was simmering away.

Sunrise over the Ganges, with the group out on the waters in a cockle-shell row-boat, was everything it had been said to be, but the visit to Benares was overshadowed by an uncertainty in

A 2ft 6in gauge train from Rajim to Raipur crosses a typically Indian bridge. Class CC 4–6–2 No 664 heads the train.

Above:
Dabhoi Locomotive Depot,
India. A superbly decorated
class ZB 2–6–2 No 89 is
officially named *Mohindra*
in honor of the local Chief
Mechanical Engineer.

Above:
Interior of the Maharajah's saloon on India's Dholpur line.

Top:
India's Dholpur line. Seen here is a 2ft 6in gauge Hunslet 2–8–4T.

respect of the onward flight (by Indian Airlines) to Calcutta, on which so much depended. In the end, some had the bonus of an extra five-hour train trip to Patna, with the sight of a BESA 2–8–0 in the station.

Howrah Shed at Calcutta was an enclave of order in one of the world's most overcrowded and poverty-ridden cities. Among the treasures on display was the first IRS steam locomotive seen, an XC 4–6–2, described by some as that 'great Henry Greenly Pacific.'

It was now time to begin the great Darjeeling adventure. At Sealdah terminus the intrepid travellers formed a 'British Square' among the first Indian crowd we met whose intentions and

mood were not obviously friendly. Meanwhile, the TCI courier and his helpers performed the remarkable feat of getting our luggage out of the buses and on to the train amongst this predatory melée of poverty-stricken humanity. Each suitcase on the trolley had a rope passed through each individual handle. However, all was well and soon enough we were settled in first-class compartments on one of the world's very few named steam expresses, the 'Darjeeling Mail.' (Alas, since this was written it has become diesel-hauled.)

A few were offered footplate rides which could only be described as a total experience; 100 kilometers per hour on this Pacific made 100mph on a British Gresley (noted for its good riding) very tame. Anyway, imagine a rocking, roaring locomotive, tearing at what seemed to be about twice the speed of sound through the moonlit night, tended by a crew of four undoubtedly enjoying themselves in a huge cab which had ample room for the six of us. It was also notable for an equally huge and disconcerting gap between cab and tender side-sheets. The writer was particularly impressed with a display of the legendary English *sang-froid* on the part of his companion, as the white-hot end of a firebox pricker was passed within six inches of his ear as we lurched over some particularly rough points and crossings. Very few were awake for the impressively long crossing of the Ganges over the great barrage at Farakka, for the group had by now acquired the trick of sleeping in an Indian sleeper! Like old campaigners, we now knew how to set to and make some pretty basic facilities into reasonable comfort, even having showers in the washrooms.

Approaching New Jalpaiguri (change for the Himalayas, now coming into view) there was an excellent view of the parallel meter-gauge Assam main line – with some action – in the excellent morning light, a bonus which was compensation for a 1½-hour late arrival. In spite of there being minus-30 minutes to make the Darjeeling connection, it appeared that there was quite a program for us. This consisted of an excellent breakfast as well as a pilgrimage to the 2ft gauge running shed. Here, tantalizingly under a photographic ban (New Jalpaiguri is close to the Bangladesh border and no one could get us dispensation there) were the rare and beautiful – but now out of use – Darjeeling Pacifics, once used on the 'plains' section of the line.

The Engineer of the Darjeeling-Himalayan section, Mr Cyrill, and several of his assistants met and conducted us personally. We had our own special fourth portion of 'The Mail' consisting of four named first-class cars – including the famous observation car *Everest* – and a van. All this took time and the three regular portions had long since vanished, coupled together for the 'plains' run to Sukna, when we were ready to depart. It had been intended to offer us the oldest of the famous 0–4–0Ts, No 777 (Sharp Stewart,

1889), but a mechanical defect meant we had 803 (North-British, 1928), one of the newest of the 24 which currently exist.

A pause at Siliguri produced some of the best meter-gauge shots of the tour with brown YP 4–6–2s and black WD 2–8–2 'McArthurs' of the North-East Frontier Railway. An uneventful toddle then brought the party to Sukna among the tea bushes. Perhaps some of the party were wondering what all the fuss over the DHR was about. . . .

They did not wonder for long as 803 left Sukna 'wide open' and we hit the 1 in 20 with frequent curvature of less than 1 chain radius that, in the

Bottom:
A Hanomag 4–8–0 at Napura station, on India's Dholpur line.

Below:
Former Maharajah's saloon on India's Dholpur line.

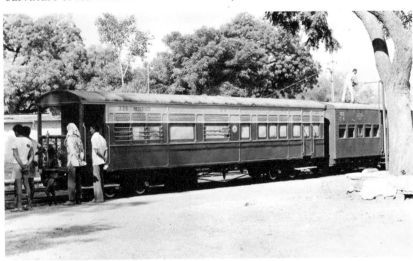

55

course of the next eight hours would take us clear of 7000ft altitude and in sight of mountains up to 29,000ft. At each Z-reverse the party spread themselves over the mountain sides (at least those did who were not with the brakesmen on the coach roofs) and at 'Agony Point' loop we had an official run-past. Tindaria works was, alas, out of bounds (too near the Chinese frontier this time!) but at Gaybari nearby we crossed the three portions of the 'Down Mail' with much flagging and general railway operating fun. By Kurseong where we stopped for tea, the light had gone – the penalty of our late start – and the remainder of the journey was in darkness mitigated by candles bought in the bazaar of one of the villages along whose main (and only) street we ran. Water stops passed pleasantly as we entertained (?) the villagers to candle-lit carols, and in between enjoyed the near perfect exhaust music of little 803.

The next day was also interesting and began with a 4 am call to attempt (unsuccessfully) to see sunrise on Everest from Tiger Hill. A fleet of taxis then began a vertical and horizontal train chase that can seldom have been equalled. The quality of the scenes meant that several people were well into their second hundred slide exposures on this one day alone. There was one man who scored 125 in spite of having succumbed (that day) to the intestinal ailment which plagued most of the group. Another was so excited by the most wonderful railway in the world that he exposed his standard 8 movie film twice! Such are the hazards of train-spotting on the Darjeeling line.

Other pleasures of Darjeeling included an evening watching Nepalese dancing and drinking millet beer in the magnificent ballroom of the Everest Hotel, while water cascaded through the roof and down the chandeliers. Millet beer is brewed in the tankard, the tankard being a section of bamboo stem – the brew is drunk through a straw and is surprisingly good. It was sad to leave the Himalayas, by taxi to Bagdogra Airport and plane to Madras.

In most of India the pressure of the huge popula-

Above:
India's broad gauge system. Standard class WG 2–8–2s at Bagwanpur.

Left:
A Darjeeling-Himalayan line train negotiates the bazaar at Kurseong.

tion with its resulting poverty and squalor – all of which tends to be exposed rather nakedly in the railway stations – is, to say the least, a little disconcerting to the visitor. The south in general and Madras in particular, is just that much better off; in fact, the human condition in Madras station is no worse and no better than that in London's Waterloo or New York's Grand Central. The same applies to the trains; no one has to sit on the buffers or on the roof of the 'Nilgiri Hills Express,' while our reserved bogie was clean and inviting, with all the fans and lights working. The WP 4–6–2 on the point was also clean and well maintained. To the writer, who spent many years caring for British permanent way, it was a real pleasure to look out as the headlight of the great locomotive bored its way through the Indian night, and admire the superbly maintained track. The way she rode at speed indicated that this was no illusion.

Full delicious English breakfast came aboard at Coimbatore; cornflakes, fried eggs, toast, jam and coffee, plus the news that the meter-gauge rack railway, which had been closed for several weeks

A Darjeeling-Himalayan line train enters the switchback above Tindaria (note the hand signal being given to driver).

because of a landslide, had re-opened for freight trains that very day. One was spotted as our minibuses climbed the serpentine hill road and several of the Swiss-built rack locomotives were in steam at system headquarters, Coonor, situated half-way up. Rides on the end galleries of the freight cars were offered, a little disconcerting when crossing bridges without guard rails or parapets.

The Savoy Hotel at Ootacamund with its excellent cuisine and its bungalow-bedrooms was almost the final treat. Some took rides on rather narrow-gauge horses and others were rewarded for early rising by the sight of a very charming baby elephant (he could only just walk) in a game park on the drive down.

A final stop at Bangalore produced not only a rare IRS XD 2–8–2 and an even rarer narrow gauge post-war ZP 4–6–2, but also much meter-gauge standard steam power in superbly groomed condition. Then it only remained to take the Airbus to Bombay, consume a superb dinner in the excellent Hotel Centaur, and thus return home by jumbojet.

Outside, we waited for the transit drivers to end their prayers and then made for Sainjees Motel. Pakistan has only just started to get to grips with tourism and the hotels were rather more basic than in India; peeling bedroom walls and utilitarian bathrooms were the norm.

Some of the party wanted another look at the station, but there was some difficulty in finding a conveyance. Eventually 13 large Englishmen piled into the smallest of Honda pick-ups, returning by horse and trap to find our rooms being sprayed with insect repellant, a nice touch as wasps of 747 proportions had been seen. The

Pakistan

The visit to Pakistan started at Karachi (reached by air) and began with an eight-hour train ride to Hyderabad. The route was completely diesel as far as Kotri Junction, on the banks of the Indus opposite Hyderabad, so necks were craning out of unbarred windows as we drew in, looking for smoke. Three oil-fired British-built BESA 2–8–0s were busy on the shunt, the clean and exceptionally well-maintained appearance of the 1920 locomotives making a pleasing sight – so cameras into action! As we left we had our first sight of a virtually pure 'Derby' locomotive, a BESA 0–6–0.

dinner of soup, chicken curry and rice was to become familiar.

Breakfast call was at 04.30 am – for an 05.15 bus; the plan next morning was to visit Pakistan's only meter-gauge line, based on Mirpur Khas, by the 0600 train; in this way we could use the early morning light. The broad-gauge pilot at Mirpur Khas was a BESA 2–8–0, while the meter gauge was very busy with 4–6–0s and others readying trains in superb sunlight. The visit to the shed revealed some real gems among the oil-strewn ballast; old 4–6–0s of various classes and BESA HG 2–8–0s were there in profusion.

Tuesday began with a road trip to Karachi and a flight to Rawalpindi; we stayed at Gatmell's Motel with its chalet rooms. The writer reached his just in time to prevent moths from completely finishing off the pillow, but a roaring gas fire made a nice and cosy welcome.

Operation Malakwal was launched at 04.30 when alarm bells rang to start the five-hour trip in search of Pakistan's best steam center. I say 'five hours,' because this was the guide's estimate, but two road closures kept us on the road for six- and one-half hours – a real treasure hunt it was at times with our small-scale maps. The last two hours took us over amazingly narrow rural roads

choked with transport hauling in the sugar harvest. By the end of this epic thrash we were all saddlesore, but there was definitely gold at the end of the rainbow, because on shed were seven BESA 4–4–0s, nine IRS XA 4–6–2s, as well as twelve BESA 0–6–0s. Working 4–4–0s are now almost unknown elsewhere in the world.

We were all kept very busy over the next two-and-a-half hours photographing six steam-hauled passenger trains, and the sight and sound of working 4–4–0s rocketed our spirits. Hordes of local children tended to make nuisances of themselves by running around and getting in the way of cameras. At 15.20 the long return trip began back to our chicken curry dinner.

The next day enabled us to re-charge our batteries travelling by train to Peshawar, accommodated in a special observation saloon attached to the rear of the train for our exclusive use. The journey took us through pleasing under-populated country with the distant frontier mountains getting nearer. A fine view of the grand British-built fort as we crossed the wide river gorge at Attock melded with more 0–6–0s, while a journey by horse and trap at dusk to the Park Hotel completed the day, except of course for a chicken curry and rice dinner.

Three class SPS 4–4–0s and one class SGS 0–6–0 'on shed' at Malakwal Locomotive Depot, Pakistan.

Couplings to the Khyber! Immaculate BESA 0–6–0s No 2530 and No 2502 headed and tailed three coaches and two wagons – with our observation saloon in the rake – for the Fridays Only 0900 to Landi Kotal. Our first stop was at an Air Force Base to allow a plane to land! The airfield's main runway crossed the Khyber line, but unfortunately photography of this exciting phenomenon was strictly forbidden. The first scheduled stop was at Jamrud, where members of the Khyber Rifles embarked complete with their Lee-Enfield rifles, to form the armed escort for the train through the wild tribal lands where even today the only law is local law. The line began its steady climb and the truly exciting part of the journey began. Riding point on the buffer beam of the leading locomotive, two men kept a keen eye on the track ahead, ensuring none had been removed by enterprising bandits!

The locomotives thrashed up barren mountain grades, through tunnels and into the first reversal station at Medenak. Then, with much oily clag, we blasted away in the opposite direction to the

next reversal station – Changai – to be greeted by several members of our own party! Changai is directly above Medenak and a kindly railwayman had shown them the goat track up through the rocks. The terrain was now both rugged and wild, meeting all expectations, and eventually we reached Shahgai for a 30-minute water stop.

The leading locomotive stood next to a water crane while the rear locomotive trundled back down the track to another crane at the loop end. Local vendors came out of the rocks, live chickens being the main items for sale.

Refreshed, the locomotives resumed the hammer for 40 minutes to Landi Kotal, a quiet and desolate spot, with a detachment of Khyber Rifles waiting to unload their supplies from the wagons before they fell into local hands. The extensive sidings were locked out of use, only the passenger and freight platforms being in regular use. For us, there were the delights of the frontier town, a confusion of mud, trucks, buses, mule trains and so on. The world's most unhygenic butchers shop was matched by the state of the

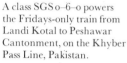

A class SGS 0–6–0 powers the Fridays-only train from Landi Kotal to Peshawar Cantonment, on the Khyber Pass Line, Pakistan.

local dogs and mules – not a place to visit after dark, we felt.

All too soon, it was time to return; running downhill, our locomotives had little to do save apply the brakes occasionally. A photo run-past was done across a very nice bridge, oily smoke providing a striking picture. To complete a great day a *mutton* dinner was enjoyed at the Hotel. Soup was 'extra' at the Romantic Overlander's price of 75 pence ($1.50) per bowl.

Saturday saw us traversing the land by train again, and confusion at the station over seat reservations made for some lively debate, but was soon resolved and we settled down in a long line of window seats. The 'Awam Express' for Lahore left on time but, with pathing difficulties on the long single line sections, was far from express. Even so, on-train catering was provided and at the appointed hour, a group of us fought our way over heaps of bodies and baggage to the diner. To eat on trains is always fun, but once again it was chicken curry with rice. To keep things humming along, a cripple and two beggars started working the train, the first such unfortunates we had seen for a few days. We were also introduced to the delight of freshly cut sugar cane freely distributed by a local merchant in our bogie. Eventually city lights denoted Lahore had been reached at last – from before sunrise to after sunset on the same train with the same locomotive.

The next day at Lahore was spent visiting the locomotive workshops (in the morning) and the Changa Manga Forest railway after lunch. This 2ft gauge system provides steam rides for tourists, using 0–6–0s from John Fowler of Bombay. Some posh BESA 0–6–0s were also seen; these work the 'International Trains' to India. They are decked out in stylish livery incorporating white wheels, red running plates, brass numerals and full lining out.

On the last day it was decided to end on a high note by going to see another group of those 4–4–0s (from Wazirabad) in action from the lineside. A high note it certainly turned out to be; five were seen, all spotless and in beautiful sunshine. So ended a wonderful trip.

Bottom:
Class SPS 4–4–0 No 2970 at Wazirabad, Pakistan.

Below:
The Fridays-only train on the Khyber Pass line, with SGS 0–6–0s front and rear, awaits departure from Landi Kotal station, Pakistan close to the Afghanistan border.

Southern Africa

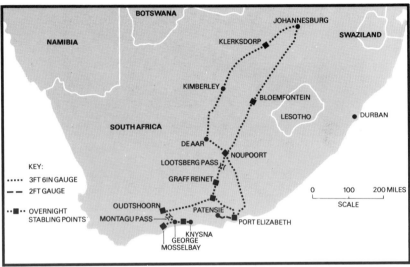

KEY:
- ········· 3FT 6IN GAUGE
- – – – 2FT GAUGE
- •·■·· OVERNIGHT STABLING POINTS

NAMIBIA

BOTSWANA

SWAZILAND

JOHANNESBURG

KLERKSDORP

KIMBERLEY

BLOEMFONTEIN

LESOTHO

DURBAN

SOUTH AFRICA

DE AAR

NOUPOORT

LOOTSBERG PASS

GRAFF REINET

OUDTSHOORN

PATENSIE

MONTAGU PASS

PORT ELIZABETH

KNYSNA
GEORGE
MOSSELBAY

0   100   200 MILES
SCALE

In general terms, southern African trains are receding in their attraction to the traveller. The furthest place north which a traveller by rail from the southernmost point of the continent could in theory reach without taking to the road at all is in Uganda, at present not a country to be recommended to inquisitive visitors. Kenya, of course, is excellent and still runs some steam trains although only for a few more years. Angola (which has the wonderful Benguela Railway, mostly powered by locomotives fired on eucalyptus wood) is out of reach after the recent Communist take-over and so also is Mozambique. Zaire and Zimbabwe are also unknowns.

This leaves South Africa itself and South African Railways, while still an efficient and incredibly impressive organization, make it very clear in various ways that they would prefer you to use their airline, South African Airways. Two exceptions are noted; first the de-luxe 'Blue Train' (from Johannesburg to Cape Town) and then its lesser known cousin, the 'Drakensberg Express,' from Johannesburg to Durban. These are two of the very few regularly scheduled trains in the world that are truly de-luxe, as defined in the introduction.

The use of superb steam locomotives has of course been a tremendous draw; even now the use of them on long-distance express trains has not quite come to an end. Some have taken their enthusiasm to extreme lengths; for example, in recent years, young and dedicated British enthusiasts have gone to South Africa to take jobs as firemen on the railways. This has been possible

South Africa's 'Blue Train' ascends the Hex River Pass, hauled by three matching electric locomotives.

because all footplate work is in the 'white' sector, and native white South Africans are not too keen on the manual labor and the dirt involved in firing locomotives.

The timetable indicates that SAR provides three classes, but *apartheid* doubles this. The 'white' classes are first de-luxe (only on 'Blue Train' and 'Drakensberg'), first ordinary and second. Then there are 'black' first (only on a few trains), second and third, these latter being usually marshalled at the head of the train. It is not so much that the grime and smuts are worse near the locomotive (though that no doubt was also a consideration), but stations are arranged with 'white' and 'black' concourses, entrances, footbridges, subways and exits, so designed that carriages reserved for each ethnic group come to a conveniently positioned stand.

Speeds on the 3ft 6in gauge are not fast; for example, the 'Blue Train' only averages 36mph for its 1001-mile run. The train from Cape Town to Port Elizabeth over the wonderful Garden Route only manages an overall speed of 16mph for a 680-mile ride between places only 400 miles apart as the crow flies. Not slow enough, many who have made the trip will say! But alas, dieselization has just taken place on this line.

On the lines which are not electrified, therefore, SAR finds itself at the present time in limbo between being a steam railway and being a diesel one. While steam lasts, this and other circumstances gives them the opportunity to offer lovers of railways something very special as regards perfection in train travel.

In the introduction the qualities that define a *train de-luxe* were set out; in Chapter V a journey in such a train as near the ultimate imaginable as regards comfort and luxury was described by Mr Carew (the one at the Manchurian and Korean end of the trans-Siberian railway). But if one reads it carefully he will see that perfection still eludes him, even apart from the fact that the train concerned has not run for 60 years; for example, the scenery was bleak and poverty-stricken and in any case most of it went by at night. Also, it may be very nice to have a train to oneself occasionally, but most people prefer company.

The 'Sunset Limited,' sponsored by the Railway Society of Southern Africa, and organized by SAR, is an attempt to reach out just that one little bit further towards perfection in rail travel. First, accommodation is wholly in first-class sleeping, lounge and dining cars and that gives de-luxe status. Then, each night the train is stabled for the night and becomes a hotel, but without the trauma of transfers, registration, unpacking and packing. And should anyone oversleep, the train does not leave him behind.

An evening departure on Day 1 from Johannesburg's great station (the third on the present site) brings the traveller to the first item on the menu – something that is almost a contradiction in terms – to wit, a South African high-speed locomotive. SAR had a momentary brainstorm around 1934 and ordered six big-wheeled (6ft 0in diameter) Pacifics from Henschel of Germany for their 3ft 6in gauge tracks. These would comfortably be

capable of over 70mph but, having bought these racehorses, SAR continued to run cart-horse-speed trains. Soon enough, the onset of World War II led to the idea being shelved while extended electrification and putting impatient travellers into the air removed the motivation. Anyway, one class 16E 4–6–2 out of the six survives as a curiosity and for occasions like this.

Most of the locomotives provided were, however, from normal service on the system and ranged in age from the class 12A 4–8–2 built by the North British Locomotive Company of Glasgow, Scotland, in 1912, to those class GMA Beyer-Garratts which came from Beyer-Peacock

Bottom:
A South African 'Steam Safari' cruise train – a class 24 2–8–4T leading, class GMA Beyer-Garratt 4–8–2 +2–8–4 behind. Note separate water tank car for the GMA.

Below:
Unrivalled luxury – the dining car of the famous South African 'Blue Train.'

of Manchester in 1958, one of that great firm's (and Britain's) last sizeable orders for steam power; a feast for the ferro-equinologist, as well as being the ultimate for those who appreciate railways as an art form.

After Klerksdorp, overnight stabling points were, in order, Noupoort, Port Elizabeth (two nights), Klipplaat, Wilderness (near Knysna), Mossel Bay (Santos Beach), Oudtshoorn, Graaf Reinet, and Springfontein. Johannesburg was regained on the evening of the eleventh day. Santos Beach was particularly nice; one could, and did, descend from one's sleeper onto the beach and plunge straight into the Indian Ocean.

Other high spots were, (i) a triple-header with class 24 2–8–4s on the branch from George to Knysna and back; (ii) a fabulous day out on the 2ft gauge 'Apple Express' from Port Elizabeth to Loerie, Patensie, and back; (iii) the exuberance of two 60-year-old 4–8–2s, out on the main line from George to Mossel Bay after years of shunting in the Capetown yards; (iv) crossing the wild Lootsberg Pass with two engines up front, one to rear. In every case, the steam power was polished like jewelry.

And what of the train? The uniform line of clerestory roofs was very elegant, and the wood-panelled cabins comfortable. Of the meals, one can only say the trip was a gastronomic treat of the first order. All praise to the dining car staff, who produced nearly 4000 of these excellent meals in the ten days.

The fact that the trip was a sell-out leads one to anticipate similar ones being regularly offered to the public over the next few years. But not, alas, beyond that time, for even South African steam is not immortal.

Left:
A class 15 CA 4–8–2, built by the American Locomotive Company, heads a passenger train near Empangeni, South Africa.

Below:
The penalty of steam operation – the fireman of the 'Sunset Limited' cleans the fire.

Australasia

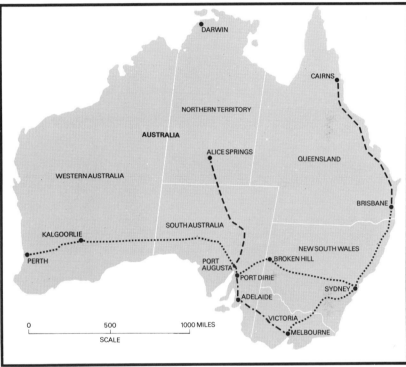

One must climb out of the rut and avoid journalistic clichés; it is therefore important, when commencing to write about Australian railroads, to kick off with some comment that is *not* about the notorious confusion of gauges in that continent. For this reason there will be no mention of the fact that, although the two main and several minor 3ft 6in gauge systems comprise 43 percent of the national network, by route mileage, they have always been in every other respect a scorned and derided minority, held greatly inferior in all ways to the 4ft 8½in lines of New South Wales (and extensions) or even the 5ft 3in wide undertakings in Victoria and South Australia. How fortunate that those two States happened to lie next to each other; it did mean that in the old days there was one state boundary which was not also a break-of-gauge point. So, to this day the 3ft 6in gauge lines of Western Australia and Queensland, particularly the latter, have smaller and lighter equipment not only than other Australian railways, but also than many other 3ft 6in gauge lines in other parts of the world; 'narrow-gauge,' a dismissive pejorative, summed them up. It is tactless to remark that (although heavy-duty mineral lines are a special case) even now they are more productive and economical, that the gross deficit per ton-mile of Australian railways gets larger as the rails go farther apart. Only an insensitive, coarse, and old-fashioned hack will bother to point this out. A bright and forward-looking author will instead pick up his typewriter and say (entirely truthfully) 'The "Indian-Pacific," one of the most modern and comfortable passenger trains in the world, runs directly through from Perth to Sydney (2500 miles). Its space is normally sold out weeks in advance; since it started to run in 1969, it has become a national institution.'

Right:
The Hawkesbury River Bridge on the main line between Sydney and Melbourne.

Right, bottom:
A new double-deck electric long-distance train set in Sydney Central station.

Below:
A class BB 18¼ 4–6–0 heads a local Queensland passenger train.

The 'Indian-Pacific' is indeed a classic train. It is beautiful to look at. There is something about heavy, handsome, comfortable stainless-steel coaches, gliding along on great coil-sprung bogies, somnolent occupants glimpsed in their air-conditioning through tinted glass windows. The feeling of envy is somewhat enhanced if one is standing, hot and dusty, by the lineside. Like other luxury trains, one buys space on the 'Indian-Pacific' not transport. It is like a hotel which happens to move. If one wants nowadays simply to get from Perth to Sydney, just as if one wants to cross any other continent, one flies. Fortunately enough people in Australia want to ride the train to make it morally worthwhile running it even if not quite financially.

The rolling stock of the train is American, of the type of the last full-flowered period of train travel in that nation in the late 1940s. Perhaps more exactly the 'Indian-Pacific' goes one step better – what Budd or Pullman-Standard might have been building by the late 1950s if orders for new passenger trains had kept coming. However, the 'Indian-Pacific' stock was built in the late

1960s, after nearly all the American trains it was modelled on had ceased to exist. In this sense it is possible to say that there has never been another train like it.

Nowadays one blasts across Australia, on one gauge all the way, direct via Broken Hill and the Nullarbor Plains: 2500 miles in 65 hours (approximately). Australia's railways are not built for speed; curves and grades and light track compel otherwise. The transcontinental line is now much improved and the days when one drummed across the desert, stony pancake-flat to every horizon, straight as an arrow at a limit of 45mph are gone. Nowadays it is more likely to be 55–60mph. Still, the first part of the route from Perth, the 400-mile section to Kalgoorlie, nowadays has the fastest passenger trains in the country, some railcars of a luxuriousness to match that of the 'Indian-Pacific' itself, which maintain an end-to-end average of around a mile a minute. One might do worse than take one of these, and break one's journey overnight. Today mining has moved away from Kalgoorlie, but the old town has kept something of the turn-of-the-century gold-rush atmosphere. Otherwise, there is not a great deal to be said about the journey. The stunning thing about what one sees out of the window is how similar it all is; there

can be few train journeys anywhere in the world which offer so little scenic variety. There are, however, parts of Australia, even of Western Australia, which are beautiful; and there are railways in Australia which rate high in visual interest. It is nonetheless unfortunate that the transcontinental run does not go near any of the first, or over any of the second. The scenic high spot, in fact, is the crossing of the Blue Mountains, just beyond the limit of Sydney's western suburbs.

All this may sound pretty dismissive of what is still undeniably a very fine train. Train travelling in Australia provides rewards in other ways: one's involvement with one's fellow-passengers, and the experience of seeing something of one of the world's most incredible landscapes. Australia's landscape is so big and so empty, and yet here and there supports a small scale of civilized life so strangely satisfactorily, that the journey does turn out to have a worthwhile point to it. Getting the flavor of a land so unusual – the last frontier of the west – makes it worth spending a few days on a journey which could be 'jetted' in a few hours.

In steam days the transcontinental passenger service was rather differently organized. Until the late 1950s the competition was not from the air, but from the sea; Australia's main cities are all on the coast and were traditionally linked by ship. The liners which plied between Melbourne and Perth were pleasant and reliable. The rail service followed as nearly as possible the same route, curving southwards to pass through Adelaide and Melbourne instead of taking the short cut across via Broken Hill. This did not then reduce the number of breaks-of-gauge; but the shorter route was so lightly-built and slow that it was quicker to go 200 miles further and get some heavier rail under the wheels. The 2700 miles took about 84 hours overall, but this included a business day in Melbourne on the way; so the 32mph overall average speed was not really much slower than now. One did, of course, have to keep changing; from 3ft 6in to standard gauge at Kalgoorlie, to 5ft 3in at Port Pirie, and back to standard at Albury (which was usually near or after midnight). But the trains had variety as well as some style. The writer remembers watching the transcontinental express leaving Perth about

Left:
In Australia's Victoria State 4–6–2s R701 and R705 head an enthusiasts' special train as it passes Heathcote Junction.

Extreme left and below:
The 'Indian Pacific' express near Port Augusta in South Australia.

25 years ago, behind a newish, vastly noisy, and very smelly diesel. It was one of the first main-line diesels in Western Australia; the WAGR were so displeased with them they returned to steam and had another batch of 2–8–2s built, which proved a better investment as they outlived those first diesels. However, the machine in question achieved motion on that occasion. It was a long train, of turn-of-the-century stylish twelve-wheeled wooden-bodied coaches; in its own way it radiated comfort and opulence just as the 'Indian-Pacific' does now, even if one seemed to hear the creaking of some of the bodywork above the noise of the wheels. There was white paint and polished brass, plenty of customers inside just getting themselves settled, and the famous piano in the observation – bar car at the back. And that is a tradition that has been kept; only Australian trains have pianos.

An extreme example can still be typical and in that kind of way the 'Indian-Pacific' is perhaps typical of Australian long-distance rail travel. Over the very long distances, there never was a golden age of opulent comfort. There was too little traffic ever to have supported it; the wonder was that the rails got there, nevermind the trains which ran on them. But all the same, there was a surprisingly strong effort to keep standards high. To this day the total service on the line to Alice Springs, in the middle of the continent, is one mixed train a week. It is, admittedly, one of the very few mixed trains in the world with an official name (the 'Ghan,' after the Afghan camel-drivers who inaugurated service on the route), and has a sleeping and a dining car.

Fairly sweeping cuts have begun to be made in passenger rail services in some areas, including most of Western Australia and a large segment of

The 'Indian Pacific' express on the trans-Australian Railway.

New South Wales, which for a long time resisted branch line closures better than most places. But with passenger flows on this remote Australian scale, the bus is an undeniably better tool than the train, if you leave the car and the airplane out of the reckoning. Yet it is surprising how much train service remains, some of quite an off-beat nature. Along the coastal strip from Adelaide to Northern Queensland, where most Australians live, there are some excellent, well-maintained, reliable trains. One can readily travel in modern, comfortable stock, with dining and sleeping cars, over any part of this route of nearly 3000 miles and still on all three gauges. And the break-of-gauge points are now no longer on the state borders, but in Melbourne and Brisbane.

This account began by rejecting one journalist's cliché about Australian railways, which has, just the same, dogged the reader ever since. It is time to reject another just as firmly. All writers about Australia tend to emphasize the vast, remote outback. But however, this is not where most Australians live; Australia is an urban country, and when its city-dwellers go out, they usually go to its gorgeous beaches. Most Australian passenger trains, therefore, are urban ones, mainly electric multiple-units, chasing each other down multitrack lines on close headways. It is difficult to think of a European city which, for its size, is so congested with buzzing, complex, commuter railways as Melbourne. But it is also difficult to think of one which still runs, alongside some sound modern equipment, such antiquated wooden-bodied trains. Perhaps New York is the nearest comparison. It is all a very rare mixture; there is nothing quite like the Australian railway scene anywhere else in the world.

Below:
Class D3 4–6–0 and class R 4–6–2 on special trains for steam enthusiasts near Malvern, Australia.

Bottom:
The 'Western Endeavour' was the first and only steam train to travel across the Australian continent between Sydney and Perth.

New Zealand

Australia and New Zealand are 'black and white'; they really have nothing in common, apart from language and what some people regard as close geographical proximity. In fact, Sydney and Wellington are about as distant from each other as Paris is from Naples, Stockholm from Athens, or Montreal from Miami. New Zealand is cooler, wetter, more fertile, more various, more beautiful and above all, smaller. The railways are narrow gauge (3ft 6in), but again have nothing in common with the frail Australian systems of the same width. New Zealanders have always set about doing what was needed, which involved running more and heavier trains faster. Their physical performance has always been comparable with the best Australian standard-gauge, and their economic performance has always been better. But this applies chiefly to the freight side of the business. Australian railways have, as mentioned earlier, always laid themselves out to improve their passengers' lot as much as possible, and still maintain this tradition. The NZGR, on the other hand, was delighted to use the war as an excuse to abolish dining-car service in 1917 and never, while the steam age lasted, brought it back; by 1945 it had pretty well stopped trying with its still fairly brisk and presentable passenger trains, and proceeded for the next 25 years to try to strangle any remnants. Success was not as great as the management hoped, and ultimately there was a reaction. The present NZR runs a very small

number of long-distance passenger trains and, on the whole, those which it does run are very good at holding their own against an equally excellent internal airline system. *And* the dining car has returned.

In the North Island, both Auckland and Wellington have a suburban train network. The former is rather under-used; although Auckland is twice as large as Wellington, its development has grown *away* from the tracks. In a rather similar way, what long-distance services there are radiate from Wellington; lines going in other directions from Auckland are all now freight-only. Nowadays the Auckland-Wellington main line has three daily passenger services: a fast all-sleeper overnight train, very modern and comfortable in rather the new Australian style, with a shower in each berth; a rather slower overnight maid-of-all-work train, with chair cars only (but also a diner); and a rather remarkable high-speed Japanese-built railcar which does the run by daylight. All these trains had steam-age equivalents, but the day train ran only during the brief summer holiday peak, whereas its successor runs year-round.

Most long-distance railcars anywhere are rather purgatorial, tending to be hot, noisy, and bouncy. Certainly this was the case with the majority of such vehicles in New Zealand, which administered the *coup de grâce* to many country passenger services. But the three units which now cover this

Oil-fired class Ka 4–8–4 No 238 powers the New Zealand Wellington-Auckland express in 1955.

Auckland-Wellington day service called the 'Silver Fern,' are a revelation, and among the most comfortable trains the writer has ever ridden. They are fast, silent, air-conditioned and smooth-riding most of the way – much of the sharply-curved track in the mountainous center of the island has been battered and dog-legged by the heavy freights. Even though long stretches are limited to around 40mph the sideways 'bang' at every railjoint is quite fierce. But on better-aligned sections these railcars demonstrate what can be done. With the evidently accurate speedo-meter needle hard against the stop beyond 120kph, they show silken-smooth riding, that the 3ft 6in gauge is perfectly all right, and that what counts more is the quality of the engineering.

The journey is scenically pleasant, and becomes majestic in the high country as the train winds past two semi-retired snowcapped volcanoes and over a succession of dramatically high steel trestles. A hostess comes along from time to time with coffee and sandwiches but there is a limit to what can be done in a two-car unit about full meals. Instead the post-1917 NZR tradition of the mealtime stop has been maintained in this one instance, to allow a knees-under-the-table lunch. And to be fair to the NZR, its Refreshments Branch got quite adept at funnelling good plain cooking into a train-load of customers, quite pleasantly, in double-quick time.

The only inter-island ferry service nowadays runs from Wellington to Picton; it takes a couple of hours to cross Cook Strait followed by nearly as long a time steaming up the long, narrow fjord to the railhead at Picton. The ferries, operated by the NZR, are combined rail- and road-vehicle carriers, with passengers considered rather as an afterthought. They are even more liable than the trains to be booked-out at holiday times. Assum-ing one gets aboard, and given fine weather, it is a delightful passage. But be warned about the weather; this is one of the most 'lively' crossings in the world at times.

The North and South Islands of New Zealand

are entirely different in landscape; the North is mountainous, but except for the three great volcanic peaks by no means alpine. The South Island is rugged from end to end, broken only by the plains sloping down to the east coast in the central part, and glaciated rolling hills in the far south. From north to south, the Southern Alps are crossed by only one railway and five roads, all that link the east and west coasts in 500 miles. Thus the traveller sees quite a different country from Australia, and one with smaller towns and a slower pace of life.

The 218-mile Christchurch to Picton line, in fact, did for a time lose all its passenger trains. Following the senescence of the railcar fleet, the service was taken off for a couple of years. Finally it was restored, using ex-railcars refurbished and de-engined, and turned into a proper train with a diesel to pull it and a luggage van at the back. To enable one train instead of two to cover the line, on an out-and-home run leaving Christchurch early in the morning, the schedule now connects at Picton with the ferry to and from Wellington, which the previous service never did; consider-

able numbers of passengers have begun to use it. It is a fine ride, through a country wild and deserted enough to pass for Australia, but spectacular as well. An even more beautiful journey is to make a side-trip from Christchurch across to the West Coast at Greymouth, a service still worked by the last surviving railcars at the time of writing. The line climbs up past snowy peaks, across spindly viaducts, and along chasms rocky enough to meet the most demanding Colorado standards. At the summit it passes through the 5.25-mile long Otira tunnel, once the longest in the British Empire. But, in the last 25 years, line changes have caused the building of two more, each slightly longer, in the North Island.

The only other long-distance passenger train service in the South Island is on the main line, from Christchurch through Dunedin to Invercargill, 369 miles. The daily express was in fact the last job scheduled for steam locomotives on the NZR, for several years after diesels had taken over everything else. It has now been smartened up and accelerated as well as dieselized, covering the distance in some 10 hours (which is good considering that half the run is far from straight and level, indeed for 50 miles north of Dunedin quite difficult). One might notice that the overall speed is about the same as the 'Indian-Pacific.' The coaches are old but rebuilt and modernized, and once again there is a dining car; the 'Southerner' is a very respectable train.

The short, flat branch from Invercargill to Bluff (17 miles) is the southernmost *public* railway in the world (the Argentinians have built the famous but *non-public* 2ft 6in gauge to the collieries at Rio Turbio in Southern Patagonia). The journey to Bluff nowadays has to be made by road, because (provided one made the Greymouth diversion, and while in Greymouth travelled on the nine-mile branch to Rewanui, a colliery with no road access) by the time one has reached Invercargill one has travelled over all the railways in the South Island which offer passenger service – with one exception. During the summer (Christmas to Easter) the NZR operates its last steam locomotives on the tourist service from Lumsden to Kingston (38 miles) in the Southern Lake District. This is certainly a train for the collector; although it cannot claim to be the world's southernmost steam train (since the Rio Turbio line is emphatically all-steam) it is certainly the southernmost steam *passenger* train.

Left:
A Japanese-built 1050 hp class Dj diesel electric locomotive leaves Wellington, New Zealand on a test run.

Below:
New Zealand's old Rimutaka incline – note the raised center rail; the special locomotives shown were fitted with horizontal driving wheels which gripped this rail. The system enabled traction to be maintained on the 1 in 12 gradient.

Southeast Asia

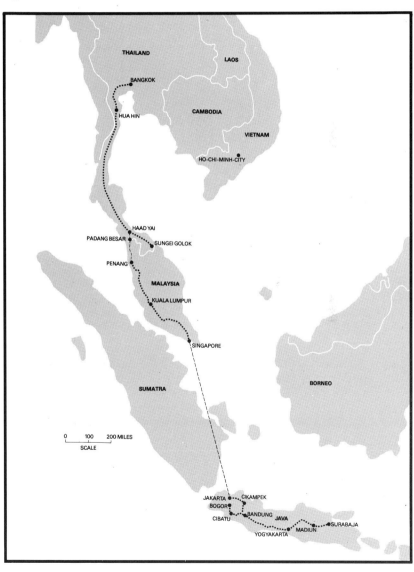

In pre-war – colonial – days, railways in Southeast Asia had generally a good press. In part this was certainly because the area was, and remains, one of the most favored and beautiful corners of the globe; here there was wealth and population enough to enable the job to be done in style. But in the other part some of the image was in the style itself, which to a degree reflected the railroad practise and flavor of the colonial power. Exiled rubber planters in Malaya, for instance, naturally would give the Federated Malay States Railways bonus points for being as much as possible a tropical meter-gauge replica of the Great Western Railway back home. And so it was, give or take the jungles, the palm trees, and a fleet of poppet-valved Pacifics. In design these last might have been as unSwindonian as conveniently possible, but they were painted Brunswick Green and had copper-capped chimneys; the coaches were chocolate and cream, the signals pure GWR, and so on. Similarly, in Indo-China the French imposed a style of railwaying which was purely that of metropolitan France, though fortunately and despite the fragmented character of the network in those days, the model was metropolitan French main line, reduced in proportion to the meter gauge, and not (as in Madagascar for example) a straight copy of metropolitan French rural light railway. Burma was colonized at one remove, not so much by Britain as by British India, and the Burmese Railways were hardly distinguishable from Indian meter-gauge standard practise. Thailand, on the other hand, was never colonized at all (its very name means 'Land of the Free'), and so the Royal State Railways could choose and mix their influences instead of having to drink only out of one bottle. On the whole this tended to mean British

A Malaysian special vintage steam train with preserved oil-fired poppet valve 4–6–2 locomotive.

signalling and American locomotives, a judicious pair of choices.

Which leaves the Dutch, in Java and Sumatra, as the odd men out, which they succeeded in becoming to some purpose. The Javanese railways, in particular, had developed a very strong character of their own by 1941. The Dutch railwaymen revelled in doing all the things they could not do in their small, flat homeland, and faced with long distances and mountain grades, tunnels and spindly steel trestles, all in rich and densely populated country, exploded into a coruscation of compound Pacifics, Mallets, twelve-coupled tanks, zigzags and horseshoes, complex networks, and unique signalling variations. It all added up to what was unquestionably the finest narrow-gauge (3ft 6in) system in the world by the 1930s, and the only one which ran regularly at 70mph.

The war, and political upheavals afterwards, changed all that. Vietnam is a story known to all, but the railways of Burma and Indonesia suffered almost as much in earlier days, in each case for the same reason, that the new independent governments could not find any meaning or direction once the anti-colonialist struggle had been won. Political posturings became the order of the day, coupled with a move akin to rejecting the problems of the real world in favor of a return to the simple securities of the nursery, by inventing and confronting non-existent 'neo-colonial' exploitations. In this dreamland, organizing the maintenance or improvement of one's own state railway system became a boring drudge, and thus a lost cause, along with much else in the way of sewerage, hospitals, education, and so on. No folly ever runs quite unchecked forever, and in Indonesia these particular follies are now being remedied.

Surabaja is a teeming city and great port, with all the infrastructure of a great trade center. The telephones work as well as in Paris, the electricity is as reliable as in Sofia, the roads are paved as well as on Manhattan. The people are a great deal friendlier than in any of those other cities; indeed, on the journey to Bangkok by rail in the 1970s the writer took great pleasure and interest in his fellow travellers. The trains, however, were not what they had been, but that did not matter.

The typical Javanese long-distance train today is made up of relatively modern and very spartan steel coaches, built in East Germany, hauled by a West German diesel-hydraulic or possibly an American diesel-electric. Except on a few trains, only third class is offered, with seat spacing more suited for the lightly-built Javanese than bulky Europeans; fortunately overcrowding is not so universal as it was. However even third-class-only trains will somehow manage to provide food en route; a small squad mainly of young women based in one compartment or in a corner of the van will contrive to produce and bring to the passenger a hot and tasty variety of rice dishes, or if preferred, one can buy food at most stations on the way. Night travel means sitting up, but trains are reasonably frequent and if one has time one can choose to break one's journey and stay in a hotel. Or it is possible to cover the 500 or so miles from Surabaja to Jakarta in a single day's run by starting at the crack of dawn (4.55 am). (By Javanese standards this is not particularly early in the morning; most people will have already started work.)

Of several days spent on the journey, a series of memory-images remain. There was a large area of green, almost empty, space which was once the marshalling yard between Surabaja (Gubeng) and Wonokromo, the main junction just outside the city; the sidings could be seen still undulating through the grass. There was a big Krupp 2–8–2 leaning over at a drunken angle, seemingly off the rails, but apparently not. A series of astonishingly high, vast, volcanic cone-shaped mountains, each standing well clear of the next, set the scene for a series of steam locomotive depots full of the most remarkable antiques, some still in action, including the 90-year-old 2–4–0s at Madiun, one of them converted to burn oil (or more accurately tar) which it was doing rather noisily, with deep intestinal pops and rumbles. A series of friendly fellow-passengers tried out their English, often quite comprehensibly. A long unexplained wait in the open country ended as we eased closely past a derailed oil tank wagon on a siding, still coupled to a little steam streetcar engine about a third its size but still on the rails. A tourist 'must' is to complete the circuit round the Sultan's palace at Yogyakarta, marble and corrugated iron, treasure and tinsel, still guarded by the Sultan's enormously aged but still warlike and dignified private soldiers. Not much steam locomotion was visible by day, but beautiful chime whistles could be heard by night. The friezes on the wall of the dining room of the old colonial hotel next to the station (not quite outclassed) portrayed the Dutch, with affection, through Javanese eyes.

The line now went on to Bandung on a secondary route through the mountains. There was more stunning scenery, but the countryside was becoming more densely populated all the time. Rice paddies could be seen terraced high up the hillside – no irrigatable fertile soil could be wasted. One small hillock in the valley below, perhaps 30ft high and 100ft in diameter at the base, had all been terraced, with water led to its summit by a crazy conduit of bamboo poles tied together. One then passes through Cibatu, the last and only place in the world with a steam locomotive depot all of whose allocation were articulated types (but mostly out of service). Bandung is a small hill town, high enough to be cool and comfortable for administrative types before air-conditioning. The railway station there is large and empty with a new and prestigious modern power signal-box; but nowadays there are too few trains to justify it. The daily train to Bogor, on the old original line to Jakarta, consisted of no coaches, no vans, no trucks, just one very run-down 2–8–2T pulling another one, dead and rodless, but with passengers sitting all over it and with 1 in 25 grades ahead, clearly loaded with all the weight it could haul. (When departure time came and the driver opened the regulator, the crosshead on the side of the engine

next to me jumped half an inch before the main crankpin started, and then the driving axle sloggered forward in the worn-out horns and boxes another inch at least before the engine began to move.)

From Bandung to Jakarta, 110 miles, is one of the better and more rehabilitated lines, with some trains doing the run in the respectable time of $2\frac{1}{2}$ hours, including long stretches at a genuine 70mph once the double-track north coast main line has been joined west of Cikampek. The great swooping curves of the new descent out of the hills is also impressive; this must have been a fine line in steam days. Jakarta, the capital, is something like Surabaja but much more hectic and very much more crowded. Flimsy houses encroach up to the very sleeper ends; indeed some were obviously built straight on top of disused, or insufficiently used, tracks. One large marshalling yard at Tanahabang had (at the time of the author's travels) simply become a tented city, with vans and boxcars standing here and there still on the rails but obviously marooned for years. Most of them had one (or several) families living in the van body, and more between the wheels, no doubt at a lower rental. Such pressure of population traditionally means squalor, filth, disease, poverty; squalor there was, and some evident disease, but much less than I would have expected, and the crowds of eager children were friendly and looked healthy and well-fed. Despite its woes, Java is a rich land; which is the message put across more clearly, but less convincingly, in the clean, spacious, modern, international hotel quarter nearby.

Jakarta to Singapore is an hour by jet or a day by ship, but a much greater distance apart in style and politics which is strange considering how much the two cities have traditionally had in common, even a shared language (Malay on the north side of the straits, Bahasa Indonesia on the south). The fact that Singapore is now predominantly a Chinese city explains the difference much more than the old and vanishingly relevant distinction between British and Dutch colonial styles. There is not much left of the British presence in Singapore, or perhaps the British legacy has been assimilated. The greatest memorial to the past is the monumental city center, built in the pride of the empire on which the sun never set (until January 1942). But the buildings are still used, cleaned and cared for.

The railways of Malaysia, which begin at Singapore, may be much better preserved than those of Java but they clearly were never, in the old days, meant to be in the same class at all. One need only compare the exit from Tanjung Priok, the port, through Jakarta, by way of a warren of flying junctions and multiple tracks, all electrified, with the casual way in which the two plat-

A magnificent 2–6–6–0 Mallet locomotive of the Indonesian State Railways.

forms of Singapore station in a few yards have narrowed down to a single meter-gauge track which corkscrews off apologetically between and entirely ignored by the houses pressing in on either side. Scenically, the run from Singapore to Bangkok has not a fraction of the interest of the Javanese countryside. The Malaysian peninsula in particular as seen from the railway tracks, consists of jungle and more jungle, interrupted by clearings where things happen – towns, farms and tin mines. Mountains are often visible but never very close. In steam days there were two passenger trains: the 'Day Mail' and the 'Night Mail.' One started after breakfast and kept going until it got there about 'tiffin' time; the other started in the early evening and had usually arrived by the time it got properly light. This schedule could be applied, for instance, to the run from Singapore to Kuala Lumpur, some 300 miles. Diesels and speed-ups have created a third train, a lightweight flyer, which leaves about noon and arrives not long after the 'Day Mail.' It might not have been a bad mistake to travel on this 'flyer' if the Australian-built railcar scheduled for the turn had performed, but it often does not and the scratch train was made up of some none-too-salubrious

hard-seated third-class coaches that rode much worse than Javanese ones, despite similar speeds on better track. Worst of all was haulage by a diesel which seemed to pour out its exhaust at window level. Passengers bounced up the length of Malaysia, from Singapore to Penang, in a dense and suffocating miasma of poison gas – not, regrettably, a very pleasant journey. Admittedly, the splendid station at Kuala Lumpur, minarets at each platform end, a slightly tarnished mini-Taj Mahal with Venetian overtones, still charmed but it would have been dazzling if not seen through diesel smog. Having endured enough by the time he reached Penang, the author chose to cross the Thai border to Haad Yai by bus.

Haad Yai is a small town over 600 miles south of Bangkok by rail; it is linked with the main land-mass of Asia by the fairly narrow Kra isthmus. One imagines a long, rather ramshackle, certainly lightly used, meter-gauge single track when looking at the map, and the impression was reinforced by the Malaysian timetable which showed a train running north from Penang to the Thai border at Padang Besar, with through coaches for Bangkok, only three days a week. But the facts are otherwise. So far as the Thais are con-

A modern diesel-hauled train running from Haad Yai to Butterworth in Malaysia.

cerned, Penang (and Singapore) are on a branch line; most of their rail traffic serves the fertile area along the northeast coast between Haad Yai and the other crossing of the Malaysian border at Sungei Golok, and four or five quite good express trains make the 20–24-hour run every day. These are now all diesel-hauled, and dining and sleeping cars can be found. But this area of Thailand saw the last stand of steam locomotives, and from the overbridge at Haad Yai station could be seen no fewer than 14 Pacifics and 2–8–2s moving around the large and quite modern yard. Within a few minutes another gleaming 4–6–2 rolled smartly into the station with a 12-coach crowded passenger train which was the daily all-stations local from Sungei Golok. Even at this stage of dieselization, most of the distance to Bangkok could still be travelled behind steam power by using a series of local trains like this one. Thus that is how one could go, taking advantage of the breaks of journey by spending a day or two at a couple of delightful seaside hotels on the way, most notably the old railway-owned inn at Hua Hin, developed when the Thai royal family took up golf; it has an excellent golfcourse, a marvellous beach plus a beautifully ornate royal waiting room at the station.

The journey was interesting enough from the railway point of view and a very energetic performance, good to see and hear, from the locomotive as it accelerated the heavy train away from a stop every five or six miles and up to a steady line speed of 45–50mph. There was more scenic variety than in Malaysia, if less than in Java. This railway line was clearly the main means of access to all the towns and villages around; at each stop jeeps and buses exchanged passengers with us. At one place the train connected with a motorboat, propelled in the standard Thai manner by a car engine on one end of a balanced pole handled by the steersman, the other end bearing a propeller. With 30 or 40 passengers on board, the boat roared off into the distance at a surprising speed down a canal, perhaps eight feet wide.

Tourists are not common on trains such as this one, generally preferring to take one of the expresses mentioned earlier. The author found himself the object of considerable polite curiosity and in spite of severe language barriers, conversed (in sign language) more than adequately with local Thais. Eventually passengers and train arrived at Bangkok.

An eight-coach push-pull diesel express arriving at Bangkok station.

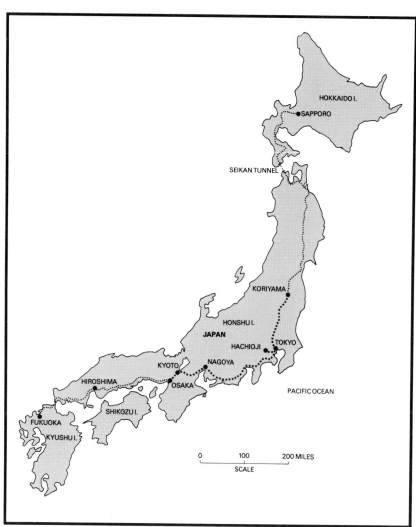

Japan had to offer in the way of railways whether they were connected with the FOCS (Freight Operations Control System) or otherwise.

Actually, the program that the Japanese National Railways had arranged would suit anyone very well for a short visit to Japan. One went early one morning to see the unbelievable sight of white-gloved people-packers pressing customers into JNR's elegant Tokyo suburban trains at Shinjuku – certainly one of the railway wonders of the world. But, of course, what the author was waiting for was his first experience of land transport at over 100mph start-to-stop, rare enough even today – in 1968 such a thing was a unique wonder. The most impressive thing about the ride was its unimpressiveness – almost none of the expected sensations of speed was experienced except that 123 minutes after leaving Tokyo he stepped out onto the platforms at Nagoya, 229 miles away.

After Nagoya there was Osaka, then the farthest place one could go in the 'bullet trains.' Nowadays one can travel on in them via Hiroshima and the longest undersea tunnel in the world to Fukuoka on Kyushu Island. High speed is achieved in difficult country by building the

With some of the greatest railway engineering on earth to their credit, the Japanese National Railways, in spite of festering problems in some areas, are certainly among the world leaders in the field. The famous 'Shin Kansen' or 'Bullet Train' railway is envied the world over – who else offers overall average speeds by rail well over 100mph on a main line more than 700 miles long, with six express trains leaving the main terminal every hour? Such is train service between Tokyo, Osaka and Fukuoka.

You can imagine how pleased the writer was to accompany a group of professional railwaymen assigned to study what the Japanese had done in the way of developing computerized methods of controlling freight movements. A serious subject, of course, but it did not prevent us enjoying other things that Japanese National Railways (and Japan) had to offer.

Business travellers today, even when on railway business, are not, alas, permitted such indulgences as a ride on the trans-Siberian railway, but at least, on the author's great-circle course over the North Pole to Tokyo, he did not over-fly any railways except Uncle Sam's Alaska Railroad. On arrival it was at once made clear that, like it or not, he was going to be shown everything

extension line almost straight (the sharpest curve is $2\frac{1}{2}$ miles radius), at the expense of 139 miles of tunnelling and 73 miles of bridging. This leaves a mere 35 miles of ordinary railway. Odd to think that if one took the normal train (which also runs the full distance) back to Tokyo, the 736-mile journey would take $16\frac{1}{2}$ hours overnight instead of seven hours.

Before returning to Tokyo, the delegation spent a weekend at Kyoto in a traditional Japanese-style hotel. It is probably enough to say that these establishments provide slippers, dressing-gown, pyjamas, razor and toothbrush but no beds, chairs and nothing other than a communal bath. Of course, Western-style hotels also exist in the main cities.

As well as the famous and beautiful temples and sacred gardens located near Nara, one can visit the locomotive shed at Umekoji roundhouse in Kyoto. Many 4–6–2s ('Pacifics') and 2–8–2s (called 'Mikados' – 'Mikes' for short – because the type was first built for and supplied to Japan) are present. (In fact, a Pacific rolled into the station with a local passenger train, just as our guide, who came from headquarters, was saying that there were no such things in Japan any more.) Umekoji is now, in fact, a living shrine to the steam locomotive, which is worshipped as passionately in Japan as anywhere in the world; many of the locomotives now held at Kyoto are in running order, although nothing is known in definitive terms regarding any program of excursions.

Back in Tokyo, we were told the story of the English engineer who was in charge of building the first railway in Japan. It is said that he made a special point of teaching his Japanese staff the elements of survey and construction, so that they should not in future be dependent on foreigners. The fact that he had married a beautiful Japanese girl may have had something to do with it. This seemed an appropriate point to ask the favor of a day out with steam. . . .

A few days later, therefore, the writer found himself, dressed according to the rules in a Japanese engine-driver's uniform – which must have been specially made since he is a good head and shoulders taller than most Japanese – drinking green tea with the shed-master at Hachioji roundhouse, situated north of Tokyo, near the limit of the suburban area. Introduction to the driver and fireman (formal exchange of visiting

A Japanese National Railways' high-speed train on the new Tokaido Line. Mount Fuji is in the background.

cards with both) of 2–8–2 locomotive D 51–1151 followed and soon enough this clean and well-maintained iron horse was swinging out of the yards with its load of freight.

A railwayman from Britain felt quite at home on a railway system with left-hand running on rail (and road, too), as well as stations with high-level platforms; once the main line was left for secondary metals, archetypal British pattern semaphore signals were added and, as we entered a single-line section, the signalman handed up a thing in a leather pouch – with a loop to catch it with – to the fireman. 'In Japanese (said the interpreter) we call that a *tab-let*.'

The glories of the 'Bullet Trains' on the new Tokaido Line tend to obscure superb and presently un-matched running on the 3ft 6in gauge. The party visited what was mysteriously called a 'Cybernetic Island' (otherwise a heavily computerized marshalling yard) at Koriyama, 142 miles northeast of Tokyo, travelling out and back (at an average speed of 53mph and a maxi-mum of 75mph) in the day using high-speed narrow-gauge electric express trains.

It was permitted to travel in the cab, high up in a dome above normal roof level and far above the so-close-together rails, listening to the assistant driver calling the 'all-clear' to his mate every time he saw a green signal – no other kind was seen.

While cab rides are something not normally made available to a tourist, there was a debit side which has left more than a tinge of regret. This was because the exigencies of the work to be done made it impossible to go further north and cross by train-ferry on to Hokkaido Island, where at that time there was much steam, including triple-headed 4–6–4s on the principal express to Sapporo as well, of course, as superb skiing. However, the reader will soon be able to make this journey by high-speed train, via the amazing 33-mile undersea Seikan tunnel, which at long last will wrest from London Transport's Northern Line the world record for the longest rail tunnel.

Extreme right, top:
A Japanese National Railways' standard class D51 2–8–2 locomotive pulls a freight train at Hachioji Junction.

Below:
A Japanese National Railways' 3ft 6in gauge express train. These are the fastest narrow-gauge trains in the world, running at speeds up to 75mph.

Previous page, top and right:
Various views of the Tokaido
Shinkansen train, Japan's highly
acclaimed *Bullet Train*.